BIZARRE Bible Stories! 2

Bizarre Bible Stories 2

"Simply put, author Dan Cooley's Bizarre Bible Stories and Bizarre Bible Stories 2! utilize a vernacular, contemporary writing style intended to reach an audience of children and youth with solid Christian doctrine and practical application. The discussion questions interspersed throughout the text are thoughtfully designed to promote interaction between parents and their children on numerous topics of interest. Cooley's books reflect his passion for providing spiritual food to children in a manner they can easily digest. His attention to detail is evident from cover to cover."

> – DR. GENE A. GETZ
> *Author of over 50 books including*
> *"The Measure of a Man,"*
> President of the Center for Church Renewal

"Paul urged Timothy: 'you know those from whom you learned...' These captivating biographies and stories will equip and encourage parents, youth pastors and others who want to ensure the enduring faith of youth in the church."

    – DARYL BUSBY, PhD
    Dean of Canadian Baptist Seminary,
    Director of DMN Program, ACTS Seminaries,
    TWU

"Finally, a book that illuminates some of the coolest, oddest, and fantastical true stories of the Bible that, when read, young people can say, 'Wow! God really wants me to be THAT radical? THAT powerful? THAT bold?' Dan Cooley does this in the simplest and most profound way... he inspires students to read the stories in the Bible for themselves. Study it. Glean from it. And then go into the real world and live it.

    – CHAD BARRETT
    Author of "Journey to Freedom:
    The Pursuit of Authentic Fellowship
    Among Men,"
    Director of Child Evangelism Fellowship,
    Houston area

"WOW! As a mother of two boys, I certainly see the need to ground our children spiritually. Dan's book is a tool to help us as parents ground our children in the Word. Dan pulls you into the Scripture and gives you a glimpse of what it was like. He encourages you to dig in God's Word and pull out God's personal message to you. There is no greater blessing than bringing God's Word to life for our children!"

– SUSAN WEAGANT
Author of "Essentials of the Heart"

BIZARRE Bible Stories! 2

by DAN
COOLEY

An **Escape** through a **Toilet,**
a **King** in a **Suitcase,** and

23 **Other Things** *that*
Really Happened!

Dedication

To Kristina Rae Barrett

Thank you, Kristina, for writing the question for chapter one a few years ago. You wrote, "Dear God, Why did you give me cancer?"

Kristina, I've known your dad since he was in my youth group back in '85. You inherited his spunk, love of life, and incomprehensibly deep faith. Actually, I think you passed us all up, telling your dad at one point, "If this is God's plan for me, then I accept it."

Hebrews 11-12 teaches us that those who have died in the faith go on cheering for us as we live out our lives of faith. If they can watch us, maybe God also lets them read what we write.

Kristina, I hope you enjoy Chapter 1.

Kristina Rae Barrett • May 30, 2002 – June 21, 2014

This book is dedicated to you.

Published by Heritage Builders

Printed in the United States of America

Library of Congress Cataloging-in-Publication Data

Table of Contents

Author to Reader

THE QUESTIONS:

How would you answer this question, "If there is a God, and you could ask Him one question, what would it be?" When speaking to students, I often give them each a slip of paper and ask them to write down their answer to that question.

When I first started doing this, I did it to get to know the students better. I thought most would ask silly questions like, "Why is all the good-tasting food bad for you?" Or, "What are eyeballs made of?" Or, "If cannibals learned to clone themselves could they live off themselves forever?" Some did, and these questions were great fun to read. But most of the questions have been tough to read and difficult to answer. I was incredibly unprepared.

At the beginning of each story I've pared one of these heartfelt questions, written by a fifth- or sixth-grader, with a Bible story (with verses referenced) to help find the answer.

There also are questions posted throughout the stories. If you are reading to your children or a class, take a minute to ask the questions and see what fun, insightful responses you get. If you are reading it alone, you can take a minute to ponder the question. Answering the questions helps get into the skin of the Bible characters.

[The Brackets:]

The brackets include background information and additional Biblical references – things that might otherwise go into old-fashioned footnotes. I tried to make it clear what is historical information, what is Scripture (truth from God Himself), and what is just my opinion. A quick warning, some of the additional information can be gross!

PARENTS: If you are reading the book to younger children, you will want to skim through these bracketed sections before deciding if you want to include them in your reading. Some descriptions may be too much for younger kids. The explanations could be violent, messy, and uncomfortable at times. Truth often is.

SO, WHAT SHOULD I DO?

This is the application of Bible story. If we read the Bible, without asking "So what should I do?" we become smarter but not necessarily wiser.

WHERE ELSE IS THIS TAUGHT?

This is a list of some of the passages teaching the same truth as the story. If what we discover from a passage really is God's truth, then we will find it taught in other places in God's Word.

The Left-Handed Assassin

The Question:

Dear God, "Why did I get cancer?"

The Passage:

Judges 3

Would you like to look different? Would you like to be smarter? If you could change one thing about yourself, what would it be?

Sometimes I wish God had made me different. It's not that I look disgusting, I've seen worse. But, why didn't He give me shoulders? My arms go down to my knees because they come out of my neck. Was that necessary? In Judges Chapter 3 we have a person who thought he was perfect, but wasn't. And we have another person who probably wished God had made him differently. But God made him perfect for what God wanted him to do.

NOW LET'S GET STARTED...

THE TIME OF THE JUDGES was demanding. When we get to Judges Chapter 3, life in Israel was horrible. Moses had led the Hebrew people out of Egypt. Joshua had led them into the Promised Land. Life should have been good, but when Moses, Joshua, and the previous leaders died, the people *"did evil in the Lord's sight."* **[Judges 3:12 NLT]** The people were poor, their army was weak, and they were little more than slaves to an evil jerk named Eglon, King of Moab.

Through war, Eglon had gained control of Israel. His life was great. He was king and his kingdom was growing. So was he. His name means "male calf," which was fitting in that the Bible says he was both enormous and callous. His army came into Israel as far as Jericho, where he stopped and bartered a peace treaty to end the war. Israel became Moab's territory. The Israelites were virtual slaves, giving King Eglon most of the money they made. In return, Eglon stopped the war. For 18 years, Israel belonged to Eglon.

Have you ever felt far from God and then gone to Him for help? What brought you back to God?

Eglon was a pain, and pain has a way of bringing us back to God. Here is what the Bible says happened next.

> *"When the people of Israel cried out to the LORD for help, the LORD again raised up a rescuer to save them. His name was Ehud son of Gera, a left-handed man of the tribe of Benjamin. The Israelites sent Ehud to deliver their tribute money to King Eglon of Moab. So Ehud made a double-edged dagger that was about a foot long, and he strapped it to his right thigh, keeping it hidden under his clothing. He brought the tribute money to Eglon, who was very fat."*
> **[Judges 3:15-17 NLT]**

Ehud made an assassin's weapon. It was a double-edged foot-long dagger, he couldn't find on store shelves. It differed from a common sword not just in being shorter, but it also didn't have a hand-guard. [One reason he lost it later.] Both the shortness and the lack of a hand-guard allowed Ehud to keep it hidden. Ehud strapped the dagger to his right thigh because he was left-handed. This made it easier and faster to pull from its sheath.

> [Stand up and pretend you have a sword strapped to your left thigh. Now, with your left hand, try to pull it up so it can come out of its sheath (holder). It's awkward because your elbow can't come up that high without difficulty. Now pretend it's strapped to your right thigh. Can you see how it is easier to pull out a sword from your right thigh when you are left-handed?]

The "tribute money" Ehud took to King Eglon was what Israel was paying Eglon not to attack them. When Ehud went to see King Eglon, he brought a number of people with him. They were necessary to help carry the money, animals, goods, and materials. When they arrived, Moab celebrated, because someone else was making them rich. That's not a bad deal if you're a Moabite. It was a bit like a robber coming to your house with a gun, saying, "If you give me all your money, then I won't kill you." As long as they paid Eglon, he didn't kill them.

Why do you think the Bible tells us Ehud was "left-handed?" Do you think it is an advantage or disadvantage to be left-handed?

There are a few reasons the Bible tells us Ehud was left-handed. First, God wanted to say, "I can beat Eglon with one hand tied behind My back." The term "left-handed" can be translated "bound in the right hand." It's probable that something — maybe a childhood or battle injury, left Ehud's right hand unusable. It's likely that Ehud was a one-handed, left-handed-only man. Only having one hand was a major disadvantage. At this time in history, farming, carpentry, blacksmithing, and being a soldier were common jobs men performed to make their living. Any of these jobs would have been difficult with just one hand.

[We don't know for certain, but since the text can read "bound in the right
hand," and since Eglon wasn't concerned about his safety, I'm going to
assume for the story that Ehud only had one usable hand.]

Even if his right hand was usable, folks back then believed being left-
handed was a handicap. In Ehud's time, even left-handed warriors were
trained to use their sword and fight with their right hand. God was letting
Moab know He could win with a one-handed, left-handed man.

[When my mom went to school, those who were left-handed were forced
to write with their right hand. They thought that being left-handed was
a deformity, even in America, just 70 years ago.]

Ehud was chosen to take the tribute to the King of Moab, not because
he was an important official (he wasn't), but because he didn't appear to
be a threat. You can almost hear King Eglon order, "Send the tribute by
some wimpy guy. Deformed is cool, left-handed even better. I don't want
to have to worry about my safety. No muscled soldiers allowed!" Ehud
may well have been the least dangerous man in all Israel. The king didn't
worry about him. He should have.

Being left-handed was an advantage for Ehud. It's the reason Ehud
was able to get close to the king with his dagger. They must have searched
Ehud when he came with the tribute. When security saw no sword on
his left side, and no usable hand on his right side, they let him through.

> Have you ever gone camping or lived where there wasn't
> a flush toilet? Did it smell bad around the outhouse?
> Aren't you glad we have clean bathrooms now?

Ehud and the group from Israel delivered the tribute to King Eglon. Then
they started the trip back home. Along the way, Ehud made an excuse to
the rest of the entourage, and hurried back alone to Moab. He may have
been praying, "God, help me get in to see the king. Don't let them find the
dagger. Please help me!" He made it back to the king's house. The guards
were standing in front.

"Hey guys. I'm sorry to come back again so soon. I have a secret message from God I didn't want to give with everyone else around. Is it OK if I go in to see the king again?" **[Judges 3:19]**

"Hey you — give Ehud another quick search. I'll see if King Eglon wants to see him."

After a scary search, which focused on his left side where there was no dagger, they agreed to let Ehud into the king's fancy room on the second floor. Ehud said, "If it's acceptable to the great King Eglon, I'd rather talk to you alone."

The king was unafraid of "Ehud the lefty" with the withered right arm, so he sent his guards out of the room. Ehud closed the door, walked forward, reached with his left hand, pulled out the dagger strapped to his right thigh, and plunged it into the king's belly. Here's the gross part. The dagger went in so deep that the handle disappeared beneath the king's fat! [No hand-guard to stop the thrust.] Ehud left the knife in the king. The King James Version then says, *"And the dirt came out."* Because his insides came out, it smelled ghastly. Time to leave!

This extravagant king's room on the second floor had its own bathroom. They used to build the bathrooms against an outside wall, kind of like an upstairs outhouse you might use while camping. Here is what we think happened. The toilet was just a large upstairs hole to the ground floor below. On the ground floor, the toilet bottom was similar to a closet. It would have had walls separating it (and most of the smell) from the rest of the house. It also had a small door to the outside so some poor soul could go in and shovel it out. Yuck.

[This may be evidence that Ehud also was a small man, as he had to sneak out of this shovel door.]

Ehud locked the door to the king's bedroom, left the knife inside the king, removed the toilet seat, dropped down [yuck, but it saved his life] to the poop closet below, and escaped through the clean-out door.

Due to the smell from the open toilet, [and the possibility of the king spending much time there in the past — my assumption] the guards outside were reluctant to break the locked bedroom door. It isn't wise to bust in on a king who is sitting on his toilet throne. Better to wait and find him lifeless than to guess wrong and lose yours. When the guards eventually broke in, Ehud was long gone.

> Do you remember your answer to the questions "Would you like to look different? Would you like to be smarter? If there was one thing you could change about yourself, what would it be? Could it be that God made you the way you are on purpose?

Ehud had an unfair advantage. No security forces checked the left-handed man. Nor did they check his right side for a dagger. The king wasn't afraid to be alone with him. Maybe God did something to eliminate Ehud's sense of smell too — just to be nice.

A one-handed, left-handed, small, smell-deprived Ehud killed the powerful King of Moab. It's as if God beat Eglon with one hand tied behind His back.

There is an old Haitian saying, "God's pencil has no eraser." God didn't make a mistake when He made Ehud — or when Ehud lost his right arm. Because of a deformed, one-armed weak person following God, Moab was soon defeated and Israel had peace for 80 years. Not bad. Ehud may have wished God made him differently. God made him perfect. Now if I can just find a use for ape-arms.

So, What Should I Do?
ACCEPT WHO YOU ARE

God created you just right for accomplishing His will in your life. In fact, He created you with an unfair advantage. He created you for this time and this place. You could have been born during the time of Ehud. You weren't. You could have grown up anywhere else. You didn't. God could have created you super-model looking. I'm guessing He didn't. He could have made it where you not only didn't get cancer, but where you never even became sick. Instead, God made you just right for this time and this place to work out His will in your life.

Where else is this taught?

2 Corinthians 12:9 (NLT) "My grace is all you need. My power works best in weakness."

1 Corinthians 1:26-28 (NLT) Remember, dear brothers and sisters, that few of you were wise in the world's eyes or powerful or wealthy when God called you. Instead, God chose things the world considers foolish (left-handed) in order to shame those who think they are wise (kings). And he chose things that are powerless (one-handed) to shame those who are powerful (king's guards). God chose things despised by the world, things counted as nothing at all (Jewish nation), and used them to bring to nothing what the world considers important (Moab). (Author's notes)

Philippians 4:13 (NLT) I can do everything through Christ, who gives me strength.

2 Corinthians 3:5 (NLT) It is not that we think we are qualified to do anything on our own. Our qualification comes from God.

Beating Your Bullies

The Question:

Dear God, "Why do You make people mean?"

The Passage:

Genesis 26:12-33

Do you know any bullies? Do they bother you?
What bugs you most about bullies?

- -

Bullies pick on people weaker than they are. When I was in sixth grade, a bully named Gary tormented me. I don't know how old he was, but he was WAY old for sixth grade. He stole my lunch money and my pride. When I got older, I realized there are bullies all through life. They continue to take for selfish reasons. Bullies want something you have. Maybe they want your good grades, your friends, or your money. Bullies don't go away as you get older — they just take different things, and acquire different names like thugs and tyrants.

- -

NOW LET'S GO MEET SOME BULLIES...

THIS STORY IS ABOUT ISAAC. Isaac was older than I was when Gary tormented me, but he had bullies — adult bullies turned into thugs.

These thugs were led by a guy named Abimelech. [uh-BIM-uh-lek — see if you can say it.] We'll call him Bim. Bim used to be Isaac's friend, but he turned mean when Isaac's life seemed to go better than his did. Bim and his friends were jealous. When Isaac planted grapes, dates, or barley, he had way more crops come up than Bim did. When Isaac's sheep and goats were giving birth, they would have twice as many kids as Bim's animals had. Isaac's flocks were healthier too. To Bim and his friends, this wasn't fair. They wanted Isaac to have as little as they had, so they set out to make that happen.

What would be the hardest thing you own to give away?

Before Isaac was born, God told his dad, Abraham, that He would give him some land. On part of that land, Abraham made a ranch, with animals and a farm. Ranching in the Middle East was difficult. The hardest part was meeting the continual need for water. They needed water for their sheep, goats, and crops. To get water, Abraham worked hard digging lots of good deep wells to leave for his son, Isaac.

They had to pick and shovel these wells, sometimes out of limestone rock, around 60-feet deep. That's as deep as five single-story houses stacked on top of each other are high. Sometimes when they dug a well, they would find water. Other times they dug a deep hole to more dirt and no water. It took years of hard work, but it was worth it. Abraham left Isaac a wonderful home and a nice ranch with plenty of wells.

The land God had given Abraham now belonged to his son Isaac. Isaac had water, and a ranch, and a place to call his own. Then the thugs came.

One night, when Isaac and his family were asleep, Bim and his friends snuck over to Isaac's place. They filled his wells up with dirt and trash so he couldn't use them anymore.

[Most Bibles say they filled the wells with dirt. The Hebrew word trans-lated "dirt" can mean dirt, earth, even rubbish. If you had to fill a bunch of holes that were as deep as a five-story building is high, and you had to fill them in one night, how would you do it? My guess is they brought over all their trash — maybe broken chairs, dirty clothes, a toilet, dead animals — whatever they could find, they brought. Then they dumped their trash in and topped it all off with dirt.]

Isaac woke up the next morning, ready for a cold cup of water and a bath. Off he went to the well, but it was full of dirt. "Hey, what happened? WHO DID THIS?" He must have yelled as he ran from one well to another, finding them all ruined. There would be no bath this morning!

The wells Isaac's dad gave him were now worthless. Isaac needed water for his family, animals, and crops. The wells, his favorite gift from his dad, were lost. This was one lousy day! Sometimes we get hurt through no fault of our own. It's just bullies.

What are Isaac's options? What would you do?

Isaac could either go to war against Bim, or starve, or move and dig new wells and hope his bullies would leave him alone. He decided to move to a place called Gerar, where his dad had dug other wells. Someone had filled these wells up too — but Isaac was able to dig them out and get them working again. Then Bim and his thugs showed up to ruin these wells too. What would Isaac do this time?

Isaac moved again and dug some new wells. He hit water — but the thugs came again. What did Isaac do?

Isaac moved a third time and dug yet another well. I bet his arms were tired. This time the thugs left him alone — for a while.

Finally, life settled down for Isaac. The thugs were gone, he had water, he planted new crops, and his animals were getting nice and fat. This new land was still part of what God had given him and his dad — and this ranch was doing better than his first one! "Good thing they ran me off," he thought, "now I'm doing even better!" He was sitting down, feeling good about life, when he saw some men coming over the hill. As they came closer, he could tell who the men were. The leader was unmistakable. It was Bim.

Isaac was sick of running. He stayed, watched, and waited. No more than three men came over the hill, so at least their army of thugs wasn't with them. When Bim arrived, Isaac asked him, "What are you guys doing here? You hate me!"

Why do you think Bim came? Would you have waited for them to show up, or would you have done something else? What else could you have done?

Bim answered for the group, "We came because, well, you won't believe this Isaac. We came because we believe God is on your side, and we want to be friends! We have seen that, no matter how we hurt you Isaac, you still came out on top. If we fill up your wells, you find new ones. If our animals have 10 kids, yours have 100. If our crops die for lack of rain, your land receives a downpour. No matter how many times we make you move, you thrive. This is too weird for coincidence. We now know the only way this could happen is if your God is real. He must be helping you."

Bim and his friends asked for peace. They were afraid if they kept making Isaac mad, they could make Isaac's God mad too. They didn't want God mad at them.

So, What Should I Do?
WORK FOR PEACE

The question we started this story with was, "Dear God, Why do You make people mean?" God doesn't make people mean; we become mean all by ourselves. God gives us life, and we can live it out any way we want. Bullies and thugs choose to be mean. That means we have to figure out how to live in a world with mean people. This story gives us an example of how Isaac did just that.

Have you ever had a broken bone, or known someone who has? What happened? How did they get it to heal?

When my son Micah was four, he broke both bones in his left arm between his wrist and elbow. Feel your arm. Can you feel those bones? In the x-ray, the bones looked like a broken tree branch, with splinters sticking out like pitchforks from the end of the bones. The doctor had to pull the bones apart, and then push the ends straight into each other, in order to mesh them together correctly. We knew what was coming, but we weren't ready for Micah's piercing scream. Ugh. We wanted to stop the doctor; we hated to see Micah in such pain, but we knew it was for the best. If the doctor didn't set his arm right, he would never be able to use it again.

Jesus said, "God blesses those who work for peace." **[Matthew 5:9 NLT]** Peace means "to set at one again," like a bone. When Bim filled up Isaac's wells, it was like breaking his bones. It broke their relationship. It was painful. Sometimes we get hurt through no fault of our own. Like Isaac, we have to run away where it is safe. But if God brings the bullies back into our lives, and if they want peace, we need to want it too. If we remain angry and bitter, a part of us will be broken forever. When Bim returned, he wanted peace with Isaac. He was sorry for his jealousy. As a result, God wanted Isaac to set things right with Bim. We need to work for peace, even when we want to scream.

Isaac forgave Bim and his friends. After supper, about dessert time, a couple of Isaac's workers came running in all excited. "Guess what?" they yelled. "We've been digging another well, and we just hit water!" [**Check out Paul Overstreet's song "Dig Another Well."**]

Where else is this taught?

Matthew 5:9 (NLT) God blesses those who work for peace, for they will be called the children of God.

1 Peter 2:19-20 (NLT) God is pleased with you when, for the sake of your conscience, you patiently endure unfair treatment. Of course, you get no credit for being patient if you are beaten for doing wrong. But if you suffer for doing right and are patient beneath the blows, God is pleased with you.

Romans 8:28 (NLT) We know that God causes everything to work together for the good of those who love God and are called according to his purpose for them.

Genesis 26:29 (NLT) And now look how the LORD has blessed you!

Glow-in-the-Dark Skin

The Question:
Dear God, "What do You look like?"

The Passage:
Exodus 19-20

When have you been the most scared?
What happened?

. . . .

Sometimes God asks us to do scary things. Jonah
was scared to go to Nineveh, Gideon to go to war,
and Moses to go back to Egypt. Following God
when it was scary brought them closer to God. And,
the closer you are to God, the safer you are.

. . . .

NOW LET'S SEE WHO WAS SO SCARED. . .

D O YOU REMEMBER THE STORY of the people of Israel leaving Egypt? It was about 1500 years before Jesus was born, and the Israelites had been slaves in Egypt for 400 years. Moses brought them out, King Pharaoh of Egypt chased them, and God saved the Israelites by taking them through the Red Sea. Do you know what happened to the Israelites after they went through the sea?

They hiked through the desert to the base of a mountain called Mt. Sinai. Once there, God asked everyone to come up to the top of the mountain to meet with Him. There was just one problem. [**"The Lord told Moses, 'Go down and prepare the people for my arrival... When the ram's horn sounds a long blast, then the people may go up on the mountain.'" Exodus 19:10 NLT**]

God was scary.

What do you think God looks like?
Can you think of any time
God showed up in the Bible?

In Exodus 33:20 God said no one could see His face and live. This doesn't mean we can't see God's physical face, as God is a spirit. It means we can't look at His glory, His brightness, His purity and live. It might be like trying to stare into the middle of a million light bulbs, or live on the surface of the Sun.

Once we are in Heaven, we will see God. For now, we only see glimpses of God. Moses saw God as a burning bush, and Paul in the New Testament saw Him as a bright light. When John saw a vision of Jesus in His heavenly glory, John wrote, *"His head and his hair were white like wool, as white as snow. And his eyes were like flames of fire. His feet were like polished bronze refined in a furnace, and his voice thundered like mighty ocean waves. He held seven stars in his right hand, and a sharp two-edged sword came from his mouth. And his face was like the sun in all its brilliance."* [**Revelation 1:14-16 NLT**] If you went to school tomorrow and your teacher looked like that, would you be scared?

Since God is the creator of the universe, all-powerful and all-knowing, He can seem scary. When God came down on Mt. Sinai, there were thunderclaps, lightning strikes, fire, smoke, and thick clouds on top of the mountain. The entire mountain was shaking as a car shakes when driving down a bumpy road. Even though we know God loves us, it would have been terrifying to hike up that shaking, burning mountain to go see Him!

Would you want to go up the mountain? What would make you want to go up? What would make you want to stay at the bottom?

The people said to themselves, "Selves," they said, "we respect God too much to go up the mountain. We know we've sinned. We don't feel worthy to go up. Moses can go up and talk to God for us." The Bible says, "As

the people stood in the distance, Moses approached the dark cloud where God was." **[Exodus 20:18-20 NLT]**

Moses was more afraid of not obeying God than he was of meeting God. He understood that God came to have a relationship with us, and relationships happen up close.

What is the best Halloween costume you have seen?

On the mountain, God let Moses get a glimpse of His glory. When Moses came down from the mountain, his face glowed from being with God! How cool would that be? You could go out in the middle of the night without a flashlight. You wouldn't need a light to read at night. You could sit in the front seat of the car and have your mom drive with the headlights off! It was obvious to everyone that Moses had been with God.

God loves you, and wants you to come up to Him — to spend time talking to Him and listening to Him. We do that by reading the Bible, praying, and simply enjoying Him. When you do that, you will start to change on the inside. His forgiveness and encouragement will help you behave differently on the outside. God's presence rubs off on you. Be like Moses. You may not glow in the dark, but you will glow on the inside.

So, What Should I Do?
. . . .
CLIMB UP TO GOD

Approaching God can be a bit like climbing Mt. Sinai. God may seem scary and distant, especially if we are feeling guilty, selfish, or foolish. We are embarrassed, so we put off talking with Him. And the longer we spend away from God, the harder it is to start the conversation. We're tempted to act like the Israelites. They said, "Let Moses go." We say, "Let the pastor pray."

Instead of thinking of climbing Mt. Sinai, picture going to God as climbing in His lap. God, who already knows all about you, loves you. He cherishes your friendship, and He's waiting to forgive your sins and give you a hug. A messy friendship is always better than distant respect.

Don't be afraid. Climb up to the God who loves you.

Where else is this taught?

Revelation 1:17 (NLT) When I saw him [God], I fell at his feet as if I were dead. But he laid his right hand on me and said, "Don't be afraid!"

Isaiah 57:15 (NLT) The Holy One says this: "I live in the high and holy place with those whose spirits are contrite and humble. I restore the crushed spirit of the humble and revive the courage of those with repentant hearts…"

Matthew 11:28 (NLT) Jesus said, "Come to me, all of you who are weary and carry heavy burdens, and I will give you rest."

John 4:24 (NLT) "God is Spirit, so those who worship him must worship in spirit and in truth."

1 John 4:16,18 (NLT) God is love, and all who live in love live in God, and God lives in them. And as we live in God, our love grows more perfect. So we will not be afraid on the day of judgment, but we can face him with confidence because we live like Jesus here in this world. Such love has no fear, because perfect love expels all fear.

King in a Suitcase

The Question:
Dear God, "Do You change Your mind?"

The Passage:
1 Samuel 10, 15

What do you do really well? What do you not do well? If God promised to help you do what you are not good at — would you trust Him to do it?

God seems to enjoy asking us to do things we don't think we can do. Sometimes we're correct; we can't do it on our own. God is teaching us that He will equip us to do whatever He asks us to do.

NOW LET'S GET EQUIPPED...

SAMUEL WAS A PROPHET. Many people looked to Samuel's leadership because Israel didn't have a king. God told Samuel to find a young man named Saul. Samuel was to tell Saul that he would be the first king of Israel! Then Samuel was to introduce King Saul to the rest of the country. Saul was God's choice as king, and Samuel was God's choice to make it happen.

Saul had a lot going for him. His family had a bit of money, and he was bigger and stronger than most people his age. He was a man of action. But Saul had a problem.

It was hard for Saul to trust God.

God wanted to set Saul up for success. God knew Saul could make a brilliant king if he would rely on Him. God, through Samuel, did a number of things in order to give Saul confidence in God. Here is what happened on the day Samuel told Saul he would be king:

Samuel poured oil over Saul's head. Saul knew this meant God had selected him for special service, and the Spirit of God would assist him. Samuel told Saul, "God has appointed you to be king over Israel!" Samuel told Saul he would meet two people later that day in Zelzah. He even told Saul what those two people would say! Then Samuel told Saul that he would later meet three men who would be on their way to Bethel. They would have bread, wine, and goats. He also said they would offer him the bread and he should take it. Finally, Samuel told Saul that the Spirit of the Lord would come to him at a place called Gibeh, where he should wait for a week for further instructions. Samuel told Saul what was going to happen before any of it happened. How cool is that?

ALL those things happened that same day — precisely as Samuel said they would! If that happened to you, would you trust Samuel? Would you trust God?

Have you ever played "Hide and Seek?"
Do you have a favorite hiding place?

Later Samuel called all Israel to meet at Mizpah. The news quickly spread that God had picked Israel's first king. People from all over traveled to see who it would be. They packed up their wagons and animals and traveled to Mizpah. Once there, they unloaded their wagons, found a place to sleep, and waited for the big announcement.

Samuel got in front of everyone and announced, "God picked the first king of Israel! His name is Saul, son of Kish! Saul, come out!"

The people cheered — they clapped, shouted, waved, and waited to see Saul. But Saul had disappeared! The clapping died down. Everybody was waiting. Awkward!

"Saul?"

"Saul?"

"HEY SAUL, WHERE ARE YOU?"

Samuel asked God, "Where is Saul?" God answered, "Hiding among the baggage!" The great King Saul was hiding in a suitcase on his first day on the job!

Saul knew he didn't have the ability to be king. Trusting in his own abilities, he was overwhelmed — so he hid. Saul didn't understand that whatever God calls us to do, He will equip us to do. Saul was still having a difficult time trusting God.

Saul became king in spite of his hiding. As Saul learned to rely on God, he became a better king. He ruled with wisdom, success, and insight — for a time.

Things were going so well that Saul started making decisions on his own.

Have you ever made this choice?
"I will disobey my parents. Even if I get caught, it's worth it. They will forgive me anyway."

God told Saul, through Samuel, to go to war against some particularly wicked people. He was told to destroy everything. God knew that keeping what the wicked people owned would cause problems later. Saul didn't do what God asked.

Once Saul and his army won the battle, the soldiers wanted to keep some of the stuff for themselves. "Why destroy it?" they asked. "This is good stuff! Let us keep it!" Saul said to himself, "Self," he said, *"I can't control this entire army. There are 210,000 soldiers of Israel here. I'm just one guy. I'll let them keep what they want and hope God doesn't notice. It's easier to be forgiven by God than to obey Him. I'll even keep some of the animals to give as a sacrifice to God. Surely then He will understand."* **[1 Samuel 15:24]**

Saul and his army disobeyed the command of God and kept the best of the sheep, goats, cattle, horses — they kept the best of everything they saw. They only destroyed what seemed worthless to them.

[Maybe they kept the best clothes, tents, and jewelry too. If this were happening today, what would you be tempted to keep?]

Have you ever changed your mind? What about?

Because of Saul's sin, God rejected him as king. 1 Samuel 15:11 says the Lord told Samuel, *"I am sorry that I ever made Saul king, for he has not been loyal to me and has refused to obey my command."* **[NLT]** Does this mean God changed His mind?

Psalms 102:26-27 teaches that God is changeless and perfect. Therefore, it is impossible for God to change His mind. So why was God sorry He made Saul king?

Hebrews 4:12-13 tells us God knows everything. We can't give God a surprise birthday party because He always knows what will happen next! Matthew 10:29 says He even knows when a bird dies. So why would God choose Saul to be king if He knew Saul would mess up?

When God said He was sorry He made Saul king, God wasn't saying He made a mistake. He was explaining His actions in a way we could understand. God often uses human illustrations to explain what He is doing.

[The fancy word for this figure of speech is "anthropomorphism." It means to ascribe human feelings to something that isn't human. One example of this is 2 Chronicles 16:9 which says, "The eyes of the Lord move to and fro throughout the earth that He may strongly support those whose heart is completely His." (NASB77) Can you imagine two eyeballs floating around the planet like space ships looking for devoted followers? It's an illustration showing us how God is always looking to strengthen His followers. Also see God's wings in Ruth 2:12, His hand in Ecclesiastes 2:24.]

God knew Saul could follow Him and become a great king. It was Saul's choice to follow or not. God was "sorry" means God was sorry because Saul didn't follow Him. Maybe this story will help.

For a moment, pretend your mom can look ahead in time. She sees that tomorrow you will be playing in the street and a car will narrowly miss hitting you. Today she tells you not to play in the street — ever. She tells you again when you get up the next morning. "DO NOT PLAY IN THE STREET!"

Later that day you disobey your mom and play in the street. Yesterday your mom saw you would do it.

Did your mom want you to play in the street? No way, she told you not to! Did she make you play in the street? No, it was entirely your choice. Just because she saw you would make a bad choice does not mean she forced you to do it. In fact, telling you not to do it is proof she didn't want you in the street at all. She did everything she could to help you do what was right. She could then say she was "sorry" you played in the street.

It is not God who changed in this story, but Saul. God wanted Saul to succeed. Even though He could see ahead in time and knew Saul would mess up, God still gave Saul the chance to do what was right. Saul stopped following God; therefore, God was sorry He made Saul king.

So, What Should I Do?
STAY COMMITTED TO CHRIST

God wants you to succeed. He will never ask you to do what He will not equip you to do. God is searching the earth to support those who are fully committed to Him. Stay committed to Christ, and He will help, strengthen, and reward you!

> "May he equip you with all you need for doing his will. May he produce in you, through the power of Jesus Christ, every good thing that is pleasing to him. All glory to him forever and ever! Amen." **[Hebrews 13:21 NLT]**

Where else is this taught?

2 Chronicles 16:9 (NLT) The eyes of the Lord search the whole earth in order to strengthen those whose hearts are fully committed to him.

Ruth 2:12 (NLT) May the Lord, the God of Israel, under whose wings you have come to take refuge, reward you fully for what you have done.

Ecclesiastes 2:24 (NLT) There is nothing better than to enjoy food and drink and to find satisfaction in work. Then I realized that these pleasures are from the hand of God.

Psalms 27:14 (NLT) Wait patiently for the Lord. Be brave and courageous. Yes, wait patiently for the Lord.

Psalms 62:5 (NLT) Let all that I am wait quietly before God, for my hope is in him.

Psalms 130:5-6 (NLT) I am counting on the Lord; yes, I am counting on him. I have put my hope in his word. I long for the Lord more than sentries long for the dawn, yes, more than sentries long for the dawn.

Galatians 6:9 (NLT) Let's not get tired of doing what is good. At just the right time we will reap a harvest of blessing if we don't give up.

Flush It

The Question:
Dear God, "Will You take my sins away?"

The Passage:
Exodus 32:1-20

Do you ever get impatient with God? I do. Sometimes I pray and it seems like it takes God forever to answer. Why does He take so long?

Sometimes I'd like to buy God a watch. I'd like Him to answer my prayers on my schedule. But God will never be on my schedule, and I don't think He wants my watch. God is who He is, and no one can change Him. He is God, and there is no other.

NOW LET'S GET STARTED...

T HE STORY "GLOW-IN-THE-DARK SKIN" WAS about a place called Mt. Sinai. If you've already read it, you will remember Moses went up to the top of Mt. Sinai to meet with God. This story is about another time Moses went up the mountain — and about the mess that happened down at the bottom when he was gone.

On this day, Moses went up Mt. Sinai to meet with God, and he left his older brother Aaron in charge. There was a big scary storm on top of the mountain — that's where God was. The people, around two million of them, hung around at the bottom of the mountain waiting for Moses to come back.

They waited for a day, but Moses stayed up there overnight.

They waited for another day, but no Moses. They waited all week, but still, no Moses came down the mountain. Now they were getting scared.

They waited for a few more days — still no Moses.

Two weeks went by. The storm was still raging on the mountain, and no one was brave enough to enter the storm to look for Moses.

Three weeks went by — still no Moses.

A month went by — still no Moses.

Five weeks went by — still no Moses. Now they were terrified! Where was their leader?

If you were on the bottom of the mountain, what would you be thinking? If you were Aaron, what would you do?

The people assumed Moses was dead. They were too afraid to go up the mountain to find him. That God-Storm was scary! They wanted a God that wasn't scary. They decided to make God into an image that was more comfortable to worship. They took a collection of gold. Then Aaron took the gold they collected and made a big golden calf to represent God.

[The Egyptians gave them a bunch of their gold when they left Egypt — see Exodus 12:31-36. When the Israelites were in Egypt, they would have known about the Egyptian religion of "Apis Bull." The Egyptian's worship of a bull may have been the reason the Israelites chose to make a calf idol. The Bible doesn't tell us why they chose a calf as an image of God. Their sin was trying to make God into any image.]

With Moses assumed dead, Aaron was the new leader. Aaron wanted the people to like him, and this was working. When we become impatient and lose our fear of God, we do stupid things. When we are more concerned about people liking us than we are of pleasing God, we do stupid things. Building the golden calf was stupid!

The Hebrews didn't see this as a false God. They thought they could mix the worship of a golden calf idol with worship of the One True God. They even sacrificed to God in front of the calf!

Do you know what an Old Testament sacrifice is? Why did they sacrifice animals? Why don't we sacrifice animals anymore?

The easiest way to remember what a sacrifice is — is to remember another word that starts with an "s." This word is "substitute." If you are in school, and the teacher is absent, another teacher will come in to take her or his place. That's the substitute.

[When we had a substitute teacher in band, a few of the students would switch instruments to make life funny for us and miserable for the new teacher. Would you want to be a substitute teacher?]

Let's look at it another way. If you accidentally broke a neighbor's window, you would owe the cost to fix what you broke. Let's say it was a fancy window, and the cost was $1000. If you didn't have that much money, your mom or dad might be your substitute and pay to fix the window for you. Being a substitute isn't easy!

Our sins [usually an act of selfishness] have a price too. The price to remove our sins is death. **[Romans 3:23, 6:23]** In Old Testament times, they sacrificed an innocent animal as a substitute to pay for the people's sins. This didn't provide a permanent solution, but it looked forward to the time when innocent Jesus would die to pay for the sins of the world. **[1John 2:1]** When the people saw the blood of the animal, they realized that they should have died for their sins themselves and were thankful for the substitute. Jesus died to be the permanent substitute for anyone who trusts in Him.

Now, in our story, they were sacrificing innocent animals in front of the golden calf. That was like saying one day the golden calf would die for their sins — that the calf was as great as Jesus!

If you were Moses, what would you have done when you came back and saw the people worshipping in front of a golden calf? Did the calf rescue them out of Egypt? Would the calf die on the cross for their sins?

When Moses came back, the people were having a big party in front of the golden calf. They were worshipping the calf as if it had saved them out of Egypt! This was too much. Moses burned the calf, and then busted the remains into powder and poured it into the water supply. Then Moses did something nobody expected. He forced the people to drink the golden water! That's like getting your mouth washed out with soap, just worse.

**What is the worst tasting thing you ever drank?
I drank sour milk once before I realized it. Yuck!
What is the most expensive thing you ate or drank?
Why make everyone drink the golden water?**

I believe Moses wanted them to drink the golden water so they would have to flush it. After they drank it, where was it going to go?

When Jesus died on the cross for our sins, He took our sins away FOREVER. Some verses use the illustration that He took our sins to the bottom of the sea, or as far away as the east is from the west. **[Micah 7:19, Psalms 103:8-12]** God wants us to know that if we will put our trust in Jesus our substitute, our sins are GONE. The Israelites sinned by making the golden calf. God showed them that He could take even that sin away, and He illustrated it by having them flush it!

So, What Should I Do?

FLUSH IT

Always remember, you can't make God into what you want Him to be. God is who He is. You can't make God into anything else; you can't mix Him with any other teaching. He is God, and there is no other. This is why God had them take their golden calf, reduce it to powder, drink it and flush it! God seems mighty slow sometimes — even late. So we try to rush Him or go around Him, or we might forget about Him all together. When we do that, we miss His best for us.

Will God take your sins away? Hebrews 9:28 says, *"Christ died once for all time as a sacrifice to take away the sins of many people. He will come again, not to deal with our sins, but to bring salvation to all who are eagerly waiting for him."* **[NLT]** If you put your trust in the sacrifice of Jesus, if you believe His death was a substitute for your sins, then the answer is YES. He has taken your sins away. Trust Him to flush them! And —

The next time you want to rush God, take that idea and FLUSH IT!

The next time you want to make God into what you want Him to be, take that idea and FLUSH IT!

The next time you feel unworthy, when you feel that God could never forgive you, remember the Israelites did much worse and God forgave them. Take those thoughts and FLUSH THEM!

Where else is this taught?

Micah 7:19 (NLT) Once again you will have compassion on us. You will trample our sins under your feet and throw them into the depths of the ocean!

Job 14:17 (NLT) My sins would be sealed in a pouch, and you would cover my guilt.

Psalms 103:8 (NLT) The Lord is compassionate and merciful, slow to get angry and filled with unfailing love. 9 He will not constantly accuse us, nor remain angry forever. 10 He does not punish us for all our sins; he does not deal harshly with us, as we deserve. 11 For his unfailing love toward those who fear him is as great as the height of the heavens above the earth. 12 He has removed our sins as far from us as the east is from the west.

Isaiah 43:10-13 (NLT) "I alone am God. There is no other God — there never has been, and there never will be. I, yes I, am the Lord, and there is no other Savior. First I predicted your rescue, then I saved you and proclaimed it to the world. No foreign god has ever done this. You are witnesses that I am the only God," says the Lord. "From eternity to eternity I am God. No one can snatch anyone out of my hand. No one can undo what I have done."

The
Wimp

The Question:
Dear God, "Why am I not like a regular kid?"

The Passage:
Judges 13-16

What is your favorite Bible story?
Do you remember the story of Samson?
What did he look like?

Samson wasn't like a normal kid. God doesn't do normal;
God flawlessly and uniquely created each one of us.
Don't worry about being normal. Instead, be faithful.

NOW LET'S MEET A UNIQUE KID...

YOU MAY REMEMBER THE STORY of Samson something like this. He had long hair that made him strong. God used his strength to defend the Israelites against the Philistines. He had a girlfriend named Delilah who kept trying to figure out what made him strong. Ultimately, Samson relented and told her that his hair made him strong. Delilah had some people come in and cut his hair when he was asleep. When Samson woke up, he just had the strength of a normal man. The Philistines beat him up, even gouging out his eyes. Later they brought Samson to their temple to make fun of him. Samson prayed and pulled down the pillars of the temple, killing himself and everyone inside.

You have the story wrong.

Samson wasn't strong because of his hair. In fact, Samson wasn't any stronger than the average person was — maybe no stronger than you or your dad. He may have had daddy-longleg spider arms.

Samson also wasn't like a regular kid.

Before Samson was born, God sent an angel to meet with his parents. The angel told his mom and dad they were going to have a son. He told them not to cut their son's hair, and to set him apart to God as a Nazarite. Their son would grow up to help deliver Israel from the Philistines. That son was Samson.

A Nazarite was someone who took a vow to dedicate themselves to God for a period of time. Usually it was 30 to 90 days long. What made Sampson different is that his life was dedicated to God. This dedication wasn't to be for 30 to 90 days, it was to be for 30 to 90 years. And, this dedication happened even before he was born. An adult Nazarite was odd, but a kid Nazarite? That wouldn't be a regular kid.

As a Nazarite, Samson couldn't cut his hair, go near a dead human body, or drink alcohol or grape juice. **[Numbers 6:1-8]** You know when he was younger other kids laughed at his long, flowing hair. As a teenager, they probably ridiculed his staying away from funerals and not drinking. "Samson, you wonder why girls don't like you. It's because you look like them! Get over this Nazarite thing and get your hair cut. Come to our party this weekend. Have a drink. Become a Nazarite when you're older if you still want to be one. You don't have to be weird, you know."

Would you like to be super-strong, like the Incredible Hulk? If you were, what would you do with all that strength?

Samson wasn't like a regular kid. And, as he grew up, he did some amazing feats, which made him even more unusual. He killed a lion with his bare

hands. He killed 1,000 Philistines with a jawbone of a donkey. He caught foxes. He even ripped off the town gates of one city and carried them 37 miles away. But, his strength didn't come from his hair or from lifting weights in a gym. It came from God.

When Samson did this kind of radical Incredible Hulk stuff, the Bible says, "The Spirit of the Lord came upon him." It was the Spirit of the Lord that made him strong, not his muscles or hair. He didn't even look strong. At least five times people asked what made him so strong. **[Judges 16:5,6,10,13,17]** If he looked strong, no one would have been asking what made him strong. They would have been able to look at him and see the muscles. He must have looked more like Underdog than Superman.

God promised to be with Samson as long as he kept his Nazarite vow of not cutting his hair, or touching dead bodies, or drinking alcohol. When Samson told Delilah about the vow, she had his hair cut. Then the Spirit of the Lord left him. He was then as weak as his muscles looked. Samson, without God, wasn't strong. The rest of the story you know.

So, What Should I Do?
BE FAITHFUL

Samson wasn't like a normal kid, and you aren't either. No one is normal; God makes us unique. God doesn't have a "human factory" punching us out like a bunch of identical pennies, where occasionally one is miss-punched, and "not normal." God is more like a master painter where He flawlessly and uniquely creates each one of us. You're not normal. You're a child of King Jesus, totally loved by God, exclusively made by Him in His image. God doesn't do normal.

Instead of trying to be normal, be faithful. Samson protected Israel from the Philistines for 20 years. When he stopped following God, he lost his hair, his strength, and his eyes. Losing everything brought Samson back to God, but it was a painful process. Skip the process, stay faithful!

Where else is this taught?

Psalms 28:7-9 (NLT) The Lord is my strength and shield. I trust him with all my heart. He helps me, and my heart is filled with joy. I burst out in songs of thanksgiving. The Lord gives his people strength. He is a safe fortress for his anointed king. Save your people! Bless Israel, your special possession. Lead them like a shepherd, and carry them in your arms forever.

Psalms 33:16-22 (NLT) The best-equipped army cannot save a king, nor is great strength enough to save a warrior. Don't count on your warhorse to give you victory — for all its strength, it cannot save you. But the Lord watches over those who fear him, those who rely on his unfailing love. He rescues them from death and keeps them alive in times of famine. We put our hope in the Lord. He is our help and our shield. In him our hearts rejoice, for we trust in his holy name. Let your unfailing love surround us, Lord, for our hope is in you alone.

2 Corinthians 12:10 (NLT) That's why I take pleasure in my weaknesses, and in the insults, hardships, persecutions, and troubles that I suffer for Christ. For when I am weak, then I am strong.

John 15:5 (NLT) "Yes, I am the vine; you are the branches. Those who remain in me, and I in them, will produce much fruit. For apart from me you can do nothing."

Philippians 4:13 (NLT) I can do everything through Christ, who gives me strength.

Ephesians 6:10 (NLT) A final word: Be strong in the Lord and in his mighty power.

Don't Mess with Little Brother

The Question:
Dear God, "Why did You give me a mean, annoying, selfish sister?"

The Passage:
Numbers 12

Do you have any brothers or sisters? Do you like them?
Are you sometimes jealous of each other?
Do you know what jealousy is?

Jealousy is thinking we deserve to have what someone
else has. We can be jealous of someone else's stuff or
their popularity or even their looks. When we become
jealous, we can get into all kinds of trouble.

MEET THE JEALOUS BROTHER
AND SISTER...

OSES, WHO LED THE ISRAELITES out of Egypt, had an older brother and sister. His older brother was Aaron the priest; his older sister was Miriam. They became jealous of Moses because he was the leader of Israel, and they had to answer to him. It can be difficult to answer to a little brother you used to take care of.

Aaron and Miriam started grouching to each other about Moses. They thought he was getting a big head about being the leader. They must have said things to each other like, "Little brother Moses thinks he is so big because he believes in God. Well, we do too!"

"You know what Aaron? You're right. He thinks he's the only one who can hear from God. Well God has spoken to us too. I wrote that song after we went through the red sea. **[Exodus 15]** What songs has Moses written? And he married that Ethiopian woman. At least we knew better than to marry an Ethiopian. I don't like her."

"Good point Miriam. He's so tongue-tied, if I hadn't been with him back in Egypt to speak to Pharaoh, we'd still be slaves. Why should he be the leader? We're older. Shoot, I remember us changing his diapers — he stunk then and he stinks now!"

What they didn't realize is that when they thought they were alone, when they thought no one was listening, God was listening.

What does it mean to be "humble?" What is the opposite of humility?

Most dictionaries define humility as having a modest estimate of your own importance, not being arrogant or prideful. In the Bible, humility combines having a modest estimate of your own importance with having a high opinion of God's importance. We don't have anything to brag about because everything we have — our brains, looks, and abilities — all come from God.

Moses was the most humble man alive. **[Numbers 12:3]** He wasn't bragging about being the leader of Israel. He wasn't proud or obnoxious. Still, his older brother and sister were giving him grief. Their jealousy wasn't his fault, and he couldn't stop it. So, God stepped in to help Moses out.

Have you ever been talking about someone — and then had that exact person show up? Have you ever talked about someone and later found out he or she overheard you? How did you feel?

Suddenly, maybe even as Aaron and Miriam were griping about Moses, they heard the voice of God. He yelled out to Moses, Aaron, and Miriam and said, "GO OUT TO THE TABERNACLE, ALL THREE OF YOU!"

All three of them hurried to the Tabernacle, which was kind of like their church building. God came down in a tower of cloud at the front door of the Tabernacle. "AARON AND MIRIAM!" God called. They took a step closer to the cloud.

> "And the Lord said to them, 'Now listen to what I say: If there were prophets among you, I, the Lord, would reveal myself in visions. I would speak to them in dreams. But not with my servant Moses. Of all my house, he is the one I trust. I speak to him face to face, clearly, and not in riddles! He sees the Lord as he is. So why were you not afraid to criticize my servant Moses?'" **[Numbers 12:6-8 NLT]**

When the tower of cloud left the door of the Tabernacle, Miriam had changed. She had leprosy.

In the Bible, leprosy can refer to a number of different conditions, none of them good. Whatever Miriam contracted turned her skin "white as snow." In those days, they would take anyone diagnosed with leprosy and send him or her out of the city. The lepers had to live in their own secluded little group away from their friends. This was because everyone else was afraid of catching leprosy by touching someone who had it. Now Miriam couldn't touch anyone, not Aaron, not Moses, not even her own children! Her case was so severe that Aaron described her as already dead. **[Verse 12]**

Now Miriam, who wanted to have the position of Moses, who desired to be the most important person in Israel, would have to leave the people of Israel. She wanted everyone to look up to her. Now everyone would avoid her.

Aaron and Miriam were both guilty of jealousy and gossip. Aaron felt horrible at what was happening to his sister. He knew it was partially his fault, so he begged his little brother Moses to pray for God to heal Miriam. Thankfully, Moses was humble.

> How would you feel if you were Moses? Have you ever
> wanted something bad to happen to those who have hurt
> you? Do you think you would be glad if it happened?

So, What Should I Do?

LIVE HUMBLY

Moses cried out to God, *"I beg You, please heal her!"* **[Numbers 12:13]** God healed Miriam, but He waited a week to do it. God knew if He healed her instantly, she and Aaron might act out of jealousy and pride again in the future. He wanted Miriam to have to live outside the city for seven days, so she and Aaron would have time to think about what they had done. God knew this would teach them to live humbly.

Is your brother or sister mean and annoying? Then follow the humble example of Moses. He didn't get into a fight with his siblings. In time, God defended him, and then Moses showed grace by forgiving and praying for them.

We need to have a modest estimate of our own importance and a high opinion of God's importance. When you feel smarter than a friend remember — any smarts you have come from God. If you feel good-looking in your new clothes, remember — the money to buy the clothes came from God. Your looks did too.

God wants to do important things through you, just as He did through Moses. He gave you just the right looks, and abilities, and smarts to do what He has planned for you to do. Let God work through you and give Him the credit for whatever He does.

Where else is this taught?

Ephesians 2:8-10, 4:2 (NLT) God saved you by his grace when you believed. And you can't take credit for this; it is a gift from God. Salvation is not a reward for the good things we have done, so none of us can boast about it. For we are God's masterpiece… Always be humble and gentle. Be patient with each other, making allowance for each other's faults because of your love.

Psalms 18:27, 138:6 (NLT) You rescue the humble, but you humiliate the proud… Though the Lord is great, he cares for the humble, but he keeps his distance from the proud.

Isaiah 29:19, 57:15 (NLT) The humble will be filled with fresh joy from the Lord. The poor will rejoice in the Holy One of Israel… The high and lofty one who lives in eternity, the Holy One, says this: "I live in the high and holy place with those whose spirits are contrite and humble. I restore the crushed spirit of the humble and revive the courage of those with repentant hearts."

Matthew 5:5, 18:4 (NLT) God blesses those who are humble, for they will inherit the whole earth… Anyone who becomes as humble as this little child is the greatest in the Kingdom of Heaven.

James 4:7, 10 (NLT) So humble yourselves before God. Resist the devil, and he will flee from you… Humble yourselves before the Lord, and he will lift you up in honor.

1 Peter 5:6 (NLT) So humble yourselves under the mighty power of God, and at the right time he will lift you up in honor.

Find Daring Friends

The Question:
Dear God, "What should I do with my life?"

The Passage:
1 Samuel 13-14

When was the last time someone dared you to do
something? Did you do it? Was it a smart thing to do?
Are you glad you did it?

Usually when someone dares us to do something,
it's either bad or stupid. We remember things like, "I
dare you to... start singing in the middle of a store,
or smell my socks, or eat a grasshopper," all bad
ideas — unless, of course, the grasshopper is dipped
in chocolate. But some dares are good for us.

I DARE YOU TO TURN THE PAGE...

BEING DARED ISN'T A BAD thing — it's what we are being challenged to do that makes it good or bad. We need friends around us to help us dare to live the life God has planned for us.

I've been dared into playing basketball and jumping off a high-dive. When my life seemed to be going nowhere, I was pushed into working at Camp Peniel. While there, I was dared/challenged to go rock climbing, rappelling, and caving. Since then I've been dared to go on mission trips and challenged to speak in spite of my shy nature. God changed my life in good ways thanks to daring friends.

Have you ever hid because you were scared? Before cars had seat belts, I used to hide on the floor of the car behind the front seat when my sister was driving!

To understand this story, we need to know "The Guys."

THE GOOD GUYS — King Saul, his son Jonathan, and the Israelite army were camping on the side of a large, steep hill. [**Mountain if you are from Texas.**] They were hiding in caves and holes from the bad guys.

THE BAD GUYS — the Philistines were across the canyon on the adjacent hill. There was a steep, deep, rocky canyon separating the two armies.

The bad guys had a huge advantage over the good guys. The Israelites had been using the bad guy Philistines as their blacksmiths. The Philistines would make things for the Israelite farms, but not for their army. This meant the Philistines had swords; the Israelites had sticks and stones. Well, they had bows and slings too, but nothing that could compete with swords and chariots. In fact, there were just two swords in the entire Israelite army — Saul had one and his son Jonathan the other.

Israel was down to 600 men and two swords. The Philistines had a fully armed army too large to count, including 3,000 chariots that carried two people each. That way, one could drive the chariot while the other shot his bow. It was like having 3,000 tanks and thousands of soldiers with guns against 600 people with two guns. King Saul assumed there was no way they could win, so he and his army were hiding in caves, behind rocks, and in old wells. His son Jonathan didn't want to hide. He wanted to attack!

Who is your closest friend? Do you think you would protect each other if you were in danger?

Jonathan had a friend who fought alongside him, called his "armor bearer." His job was to protect Jonathan by carrying his shield. The armor bearer also would carry extra weapons for Jonathan. Jonathan went to his armor bearer to talk him into attacking the entire Philistine army with him — just the two of them against thousands! His words were, *"Perhaps the Lord will act in our behalf. Nothing can hinder the Lord from saving, whether by many or by few."* **[1 Sam 14:6 NLT]** I don't know about you, but I'd want to hear more of a plan than "perhaps" before attacking a few thousand Philistines. The poor armor bearer didn't even have a sword.

If you were Jonathan, there were a number of reasons to stay hidden in a cave. The King, your dad, wasn't going to fight. You were wildly outnumbered. It wasn't logical to pick a fight. You were young — way too young to want to die. But Jonathan believed God wanted him to go.

If you were the armor bearer, would you go with Jonathan? What are some good reasons not to go? What are some reasons to go?

The armor bearer must have thought, "Jonathan has been a great friend. He seems to walk with God. Maybe God really will step in and help. If this works, it would be the coolest story ever, and I'll be a hero! YES! If this doesn't work and we die, well, the Philistines will probably kill us all in a few days anyway."

"Hey Jonathan — Let's go!"

When they got to the canyon between the mountains, Jonathan let the Philistines see them. This was lousy military strategy, as they lost the chance to surprise the enemy. But Jonathan had an idea he believed was more important than strategy.

Jonathan asked God to speak through the Philistines. Jonathan wasn't certain yet if God wanted him to fight the Philistines or not. This gave God a chance to tell him what to do. First, Jonathan would yell up at the Philistines. If the Philistines said to go away, they would. If they said to come on up, they would go up. God knew Jonathan's plan. If He wanted to stop Jonathan, all God had to do was have the Philistines yell down the hill, "Go away you gravy-sucking Israelite!" **[I know how I'd be praying if I was the armor bearer.]**

When the Philistines saw them climbing in the canyon they made fun of them. "Look, they are crawling out of their holes!" Then they yelled something I wouldn't have wanted to hear if I was the armor bearer. "Come on up here, and we'll teach you a lesson!" they shouted.

That was all Jonathan needed to hear. "The Lord will help us!" he told his armor bearer, and climb up is what they did.

They had to climb hand over hand to get to the top of the cliff. You can imagine Jonathan and his armor bearer poking their heads over the top of the cliff and seeing nothing but the soldiers' boots. Swinging his sword at their ankles, Jonathan clambered over the top. He and his armor bearer went to war against the entire Philistine army! Then God stepped in. An earthquake shook the ground. The 6,000 chariot drivers and shooters panicked. The Philistines started going batty, even killing each other in their fear. Jonathan and his armor bearer conquered an army of thousands with one sword and God on their side. You know the armor bearer told that story to his grandkids — "Yup, that was me. Armor bearer, super-warrior!"

So, What Should I Do?
FIND DARING FRIENDS

A God-sized adventure begins when we seize the opportunities God gives us. People who seize opportunities don't have all the answers, but they don't sit around waiting for them either. No one wants to be stuck on the side of a mountain outnumbered and outgunned. Following God's will for you isn't always easy, secure, or comfortable. But it will be exciting.

Sometimes we are in a spot where we want to climb into a cave, or our bedroom, and hide. God wants you to know you are undeniably useful. You can do great things through Him. One way to make sure we are following Him is to have daring friends who love God.

What should you do with your life? First, accept Jesus as your Lord and Savior. That means you accept that He died for your sins and can wash away all the wrong you have ever done. Then, read the Bible and follow

Him as Lord wherever He leads. Lastly, find Godly, daring friends. You won't regret it, and you just may have stories to tell to your grandkids. A daring adventure will begin when you seize the opportunities God gives you.

Where else is this taught?

Daniel 3:16-18 (MSG) Shadrach, Meshach, and Abednego answered King Nebuchadnezzar, "Your threat means nothing to us. If you throw us in the fire, the God we serve can rescue us from your roaring furnace and anything else you might cook up, O king. But even if he doesn't, it wouldn't make a bit of difference, O king. We still wouldn't serve your gods or worship the gold statue you set up."

Hebrews 11:1-2 (MSG) The fundamental fact of existence is that this trust in God, this faith, is the firm foundation under everything that makes life worth living. It's our handle on what we can't see. The act of faith is what distinguished our ancestors, set them above the crowd.

Hebrews 11:7 (MSG) By faith, Noah built a ship in the middle of dry land. He was warned about something he couldn't see and acted on what he was told. The result? His family was saved. His act of faith drew a sharp line between the evil of the unbelieving world and the rightness of the believing world. As a result, Noah became intimate with God.

Hebrews 11:32-35 (MSG) I could go on and on, but I've run out of time. There are so many more — Gideon, Barak, Samson, Jephthah, David, Samuel, the prophets ... Through acts of faith, they toppled kingdoms, made justice work, took the promises for themselves. They were protected from lions, fires, and sword thrusts, turned disadvantage to advantage, won battles, routed alien armies. Women received their loved ones back from the dead. There were those who, under torture, refused to give in and go free, preferring something better: resurrection.

Luke 9:23 (NLT) Then he said to the crowd, "If any of you wants to be my follower, you must turn from your selfish ways, take up your cross daily, and follow me."

The Crazy Actor

The Question:

Dear God, "Why did You make my life so horrible? WHY ME?"

The Passage:

1 Samuel 21

Has there ever been a day when your life felt horrible? What happened?

God allows you to go through hard times so you can learn to rely on Him. God will rescue you, He will protect you, He won't drop you — no matter how bad things seem. We often learn more through difficult times than we do when life is easy.

HARD TIMES COMING...

M AYBE IF I ACT INSANE they won't kill me," thought David. So he started acting like a dog needing to be let outside. This was David's horrible day.

Sometimes the worst days seem to come after the best days.

King David grew up in a family with seven older brothers. As the youngest, David was stuck being the shepherd for his family when his brothers grew up, left home, or had to go off to war. His dad was probably old by the time David was a young teenager, so he needed David's help. They owned sheep and goats, which David would take to the neighboring valleys to graze. It must have been a loud, chaotic, wild home to grow up in with seven brothers, older parents, and a bunch of animals. When David had to leave home, his life really went weird.

We don't know the exact time line of David's life, but here is a rough calculation of what it may have looked like.

GRADE SIX: David grew up learning in his dad's school of shepherding. When he was in about sixth grade, the prophet Samuel showed up at his house and anointed him to be the next king of Israel.

This was awkward, because his best friend was Prince Jonathan. Jonathan was King Saul's son, so the nation expected Jonathan to be the next king. Samuel said David would be king instead. Somehow, David and Jonathan remained friends even though both knew there could be only one king in the future.

AGE 13: David loved music. Perhaps he enjoyed playing music and singing while taking care of the sheep and goats. It might be easier to learn to sing around animals than humans. They don't complain as much. Besides, what else do you do out on a hillside without electricity? David had a natural ability in music. The Bible book of Psalms includes many of the songs he wrote.

David was only about 13 years old when King Saul heard what a great musician he had become. Saul brought David into the palace as his personal singer. David didn't live at the palace all the time; he was more like Saul's favorite one-man band who would come and play at the king's request. **[1 Samuel 16:17, 1 Samuel 17:15]** This gave David time to spend with his friend Jonathan, Saul's son. It also was a welcome break from watching the flocks, where he still spent most of his time. Who wouldn't want to take a break from work to spend time with your best friend in the palace?

AGE 14: David was maybe 14 when he started watching the flocks alone. This was dangerous work. Rustlers would try to sneak in and steal the sheep. Lions and bears would try to come in and eat the sheep. Poisonous snakes could kill a lamb or a shepherd with one strike. David's brothers and dad would have taught him how to use a shepherd's staff, rod, and sling, among other weapons. His training might have gone something like this:

"OK, David, grab your staff. That hooked end you've used to move the sheep before. Now let's talk about that straight end. You can use that like a spear to jab at wild dogs or wolves to keep them away from the sheep. But I brought you here for another reason. There is a nest of saw-scaled vipers by that rock wall. Let's go see you smash one with the flat end of your staff. These vipers are aggressive, so smash him hard!"

SMASH, "Did I do it?"

"I think ... No, look out, HE'S COMING AT YOU! Now smash that viper's head!"

SMASH. SMASH. SMASH. SMASH. SMASH. "How about now? I killed him good, eh big brother? What do you think, Eliab?"

"Nice job, David. It looks like someone dropped a barn on him. Now for the sling; you've gotten extremely accurate with yours. Just remember to keep a few stones with you, and keep practicing. You never know when you may need it!" [A sling was **NOT** a slingshot; it was the most effective long-range weapon of warfare of the time, with a longer range even than bows and arrows until the longbow was developed.]

One day a lion rushed in and attacked a lamb. God enabled David to attack and kill the lion, saving the lamb. Another time a bear came in to take an animal, and David killed the bear! How cool is it to know God could give you the power to kill a lion or a bear without a gun?

AGE 16: David was likely in his mid-teens when his dad asked him to take a break from watching the flocks. His brothers were soldiers in the army, and Dad needed David to bring them food. When David met his brothers and King Saul at the battlefront, he heard the giant Goliath mocking the army. Goliath had been doing this for 40 days, and no one was brave enough to fight him. He was so big that if he had played basketball and stood under a basketball basket, his head would have been inside the hoop! David said to himself, "Self," he said, "if God could enable me to kill a bear and a lion, God could help me defeat Goliath too." [Goliath was 9 feet 9 inches tall if measured by the 18-inch cubit.]

David attacked and killed Goliath, and his fame began to spread. At 16, who wouldn't want to go back to school as the first-ever teenage war hero? [1 Samuel 17]

AGE 20: When David was about college aged for us, he became the armor bearer to Saul. This put David in the important position of protecting the king with his life. If you have to go to war, you may as well serve next to the most powerful man in the country.

AGE 25: Have you ever had a good friend who suddenly stopped being your friend? That's what happened to David. In the previous five years, King Saul had started becoming envious of David.

Saul said to himself, "Self," he said, "what gives David the right to think he should be the next king? My son Jonathan should be the next king! They are singing about how I've killed thousands of Philistines but David has killed tens of thousands. Who taught these songwriters how to count? I'd better get rid of David before he takes the throne from me — or from Jonathan! It can't look like I'm killing him on purpose. Maybe he could die in battle. The little jerk — it would serve him right."

Saul made David the commander of a thousand troops when he was just in his mid-20s. Most likely Saul did it so David would die in battle. If that was Saul's hope, it didn't work. Just like with the bear, the lion, and Goliath, God enabled David to win even more battles. He was even more popular now! But not with Saul. [1 Samuel 18:7-13]

AGE 27: David was about 27 when he married Michal. David married well. Michal had a cool name, and she was the king's daughter. If you are going to get married, you may as well choose a princess. [1 Samuel 18:21-28]

AGE 29: When David hit 29, his life changed. Sometimes the worst days come after the best days.

Do you think you would have enjoyed being David from birth to age 27? What would you like about it? What would you not like?

King Saul went from being envious of David to going spine-chilling vicious. Satan put in Saul's heart the compulsion to kill David. David heard the news and ran for his life. David had no troops. He had no family with him. Jonathan couldn't help because he was back at the palace with his wacko father. If David went back home to his wife Michal, they would both be in danger. David was alone. Sometimes the worst days seem to come after the best days. And this day wasn't over yet.

Without knowing where else to go, David ran to the temple. The priest was able to help him with some food. David asked, "Do you have any weapons? I had to leave so quickly, I have no sword or shield." The huge sword that had once belonged to Goliath was stored in the temple, so the priest gave it to David. Now David had to run — but where could he go? He must have felt as if his life was horrible. It was about to get worse.

What was your worst day ever? If you could do that day over again, is there anything you would do differently?

It would have been easy for David to ask, "Why me?" He had spent his life killing bears and giants, fighting wars and writing songs. He wasn't used to loss. On this day, he lost everything. He couldn't go back to his parents or wife or brothers or his best friend. That would put them in danger from King Saul, who was already looking for David in those places. David panicked and ran to the most foolish place, the most dangerous place you could imagine.

Taking Goliath's sword with him, David ran to Goliath's hometown of Gath! It wasn't long before the Philistine officers told King Achish of Gath who David was. You can't be that popular and not be recognized. Now David was in a mess. This day had gone from bad to worse to horrible. First King Saul wanted to kill him. Then he was stuck in Gath with Goliath's sword awkwardly hanging around his side. Finally, the officers identified David as the killer of tens of thousands of Philistines. It was time to kill David, the Goliath killer, in Goliath's hometown of Gath — and they could even use Goliath's sword!

David must have felt like a goldfish when it jumps out of its bowl into the cat's dinner dish. David the giant-killer, David anointed to become the next king of Israel, David married to the princess, David best friend to King Saul's son Jonathan, David killer of bears and lions — this same David pretended to be insane.

David knew the Philistines believed you shouldn't do anything bad to a crazy person. If you did, the Philistines thought the gods would then do bad things to you — maybe even make you go crazy. So, David got down on all fours like a dog and started scratching on the doors. He began drooling like a dog, so that drool was running down his beard. Can you imagine him panting and drooling and scratching, acting as crazy as possible so there could be no way they would think he was normal? Inside he must have been thinking, "Why me?"

How would 29 great years, before this bad time, make this time seem worse?

The Philistines believed David's act, so they kicked him out of town without killing him. David ran to the wilderness. There God sent him his friends and relatives. It would take about six more years before Saul died and David became king of Israel. David would remain king until his death at about 75 years old.

This bad day was the beginning of six difficult years for David. He was a fugitive and an outlaw in his own country. He must have asked himself many times, "Why is life so horrible — why me?" David couldn't have known what God knew. God knew these six years were necessary to develop David into the greatest king in the history of Israel.

During this time, David became a bit of a folk hero. He used the Cave of Adullam as his headquarters, and he had the sword of Goliath as his personal weapon. Six hundred men came and joined him. He became a military strategist, a general, and a mayor over this little city of discontents. Some of those who came and joined him became his closest friends and helped him lead Israel when he became king.

So, What Should I Do?

RELY ON GOD IN THE HARD TIMES

God allows you to go through hard times because you can learn to rely on Him in difficult circumstances. He will rescue you, He will protect you, He won't drop you — no matter how bad things seem. We can learn through good times too, especially as we spend time in His Word. But, we often learn more through difficult times than we do when life is easy.

David wrote a song about this hard time in Psalms 34. One line in it is, "Taste and see that the Lord is good. Oh, the joys of those who take refuge in him!" **[Psalms 34:8]**

Where else is this taught?

This is the Psalm David wrote about the day he acted crazy:

Psalms 34:1-10 (NLT) I will praise the Lord at all times. I will constantly speak his praises. I will boast only in the Lord; let all who are helpless take heart. Come, let us tell of the Lord's greatness; let us exalt his name together. I prayed to the Lord, and he answered me. He freed me from all my fears. Those who look to him for help will be radiant with joy; no shadow of shame will darken their faces. In my desperation I prayed, and the Lord listened; he saved me from all my troubles. For the angel of the Lord is a guard; he surrounds and defends all who fear him. Taste and see that the Lord is good. Oh, the joys of those who take refuge in him! Fear the Lord, you his godly people, for those who fear him will have all they need. Even strong young lions sometimes go hungry, but those who trust in the Lord will lack no good thing.

Matthew 6:34 (NLT) So don't worry about tomorrow, for tomorrow will bring its own worries. Today's trouble is enough for today.

2 Corinthians 1:8-9 (NLT) We think you ought to know, dear brothers and sisters, about the trouble we went through in the province of Asia. We were crushed and overwhelmed beyond our ability to endure, and we thought we would never live through it. In fact, we expected to die. But as a result, we stopped relying on ourselves and learned to rely only on God, who raises the dead.

God's Masterpiece

The Question:
Dear God, "Why do You spare us when we sin really badly?"

The Passage:
1 Samuel 5-6

Have you ever sinned really badly?
Do you think God can forgive you?

Moses committed murder. The disciples ran from Jesus the night He needed them the most. Jonah just ran. Jacob had a problem with lying; Noah with drinking; Jeremiah with depression; and Lazarus completely blew it. He died.

WARNING: PLAGUES, RATS, AND FLIES COMING...

GOD SPARES US WHEN WE sin really badly because He still wants to use us. Moses led the Israelites out of Egypt after he committed murder. The disciples started the church after running away. Jonah led the greatest revival in history after getting thrown-up by the fish. And Lazarus — he came back to life after death so God could finish what He called him to do. You may have blown it, but you're not dead yet.

About 1,000 years before Jesus was born, an army of Philistines stole something from the Israelites. They stole the Ark. The Ark was an extraordinary box about 4-feet long by 2-feet wide and high. God had the Israelites make the Ark out of wood covered with gold. We think the lid, called the "mercy seat," was solid gold. Inside the box was (any guesses?) the real, written on stone by God Himself — Ten Commandments! Of all the things Israel owned, the Ark was their favorite.

[If you have a yardstick or tape measure, you can figure out how large it was. It's about the size of a coffee table, but a little taller. The movie "Raiders of the Lost Ark" used a fairly accurate replica.]

One day they brought the Ark into battle against the Philistines, thinking it would help them win the battle. [Dumb move.] It didn't. Instead, the Philistines nabbed it. They were bullies and they wanted to take Israel's most favorite stuff. [Dumber move.]

What the Philistines didn't know is that God is real. God gave the Ark and the Commandments to Israel. He wanted them to have it. When the Philistines stole the Ark, they upset God. God loves His people, and when He gives us a gift, He doesn't want others stealing it.

Have you ever made someone mad who is bigger than you are? What happened?

The Philistines said to themselves, "Selves," they said. "what should we do with this big gold box?" Maybe the guys wanted to melt the lid down for gold chariot wheels, the women wanted earrings. To keep it safe until the women won the argument, they ended up storing it with their idol Dagon in his temple. That was a mistake. When they went in the temple the next day, Dagon was off his pedestal, bowing before the Ark!

The town's people didn't know what to make of this. Had someone come in and moved the idol? How else could it happen? The next night they secured Dagon on his pedestal and made the Dagon Temple secure. When they came in the next day, Dagon was bowing before the Ark again, this time with his head and hands broken off! God was warning the people that He was real, Dagon wasn't, and He wanted the Ark back.

The Philistines weren't listening. They didn't want to give the Ark back, so they moved it into a different storage facility in Ashdod.

God hit the people of Ashdod with a plague of tumors and death. The town leaders sent the Ark to Gath. God hit Gath with the plague. Someone must have had a wicked stepmother in Ekron, so the Philistines sent the Ark to Ekron. Plague city. They sent it to five cities before giving up.

Wherever the Philistines kept the Ark, rats and fleas appeared. The people became sick, and many died. Rats scurried in the streets, slid under doors and into kitchen cupboards.

They spread disease from house to house. If you could avoid the rats — you were stuck with the fleas. Nasty, biting fleas would get into your bed. Fleas were buzzing, rats were scurrying, and the Ark was waiting to go home. [We know a disease, which resulted in tumors, went wherever the Ark went, but the rats aren't mentioned until later in the passage.]

When the people in town became sick, they developed tumors. Do you know what a tumor is? A tumor is a lump on your body that isn't supposed to be there. In all probability, what the Philistines had is a disease called "bubonic plague." It's sometimes called "black death," because it causes black spots on the skin and tumors on the body. Yuck.

[I'm told the lymph nodes swell, especially in the area of the armpit or groin. This is most likely what was referred to as the "tumors," a word which means "mound" in Hebrew.]

Fleas spread the bubonic plague from rats to humans. The rats have the disease; biting the rats spreads the plague to the fleas. Then the infected fleas bite people, giving them the disease. Back then, once the plague started, it was almost impossible to stop. The disease would have spread fast, with four out of five people who got the disease dying within eight days! Ouch! [This is the average mortality rate for the plague if left untreated.]

[The fleas pick up the disease and it blocks their stomach. That makes them super hungry, so they bite rats and people even more. When they bite people, they can't swallow, so they regurgitate now infected blood with the plague back into the wound. Yuck!]

God must have been outraged with the Philistines to give them black death!

The Philistines were so stubborn; they let this happen in five cities. Each time the Ark showed up in a city, so did the rats, the fleas, the tumors, the plague and death. Everywhere the Ark went, black death followed. For seven months, the Philistines kept the Ark. That's as long as from when school gets out for summer break until Christmas. Why did they keep it for so long? They didn't believe the God of the Ark could cause the disease. [How many days is that? Over 200 days of death!]

If you were the ruler of a Philistine city with the Ark, what would you do? Have you ever done something bad and tried to make it right? What was it?

After seven months, the Philistines wised up. They said, "We gotta get rid of this Ark! Everywhere it goes there are rats, fleas, disease, and death. Maybe it's coincidence, but then again maybe their God is real. How should we get rid of it?"

They asked their priests of Dagon, "What should we do with the box? We can't trash it — their God might come after us. We can't keep it. It gives us tumors. We can't just take it back — the Israelites would kill us when they see us coming. What should we do?" Their priests had some strange advice.

What do you think they should do? If you were going to give God a present, what would you give Him?

The priests said, "Here's what you need to do. Find a couple of cows that have never pulled a cart — so they won't know how to pull one. Also, pick cows that have recently had calves — so they will want to go home to their babies. Then build a brand new cart and secure the Ark on it. When you're done, hitch the cows that don't know how to pull a cart to the cart. Leave the calves in the barn, so the cows will want to go back to their babies. Then stand back and see if the cows can pull the cart. If the cows run back to their calves in the barn, we'll know the Ark is just a normal box. If the cows get frustrated at each other because they don't know how to pull a cart and wander around bumping into each other, we'll know the Ark is just a normal box. But, if a miracle happens, and the cows can pull the cart, and they pull it to Israel instead of to their calves back in the barn, then get out of the way! We'll know there is a God in Israel. He loves his people and we stole from them. We won't mess with Him anymore!"

The Philistine leaders felt a little guilty about stealing the Ark in the first place, so they wanted to give God a present when they sent the Ark back. [In verse 4 "trespass offering" means "guilt or sin offering."] What could they give God to show Him they were sorry for taking the Ark? The best gift God wants from us — is us! He wants us to love and obey Him. Did the Philistines give their lives to God? Well, no. They felt guilty, but not that guilty. Instead, they decided to give God 10 expensive, ugly presents. What do you think they were?

They made five gold rats and five gold tumors for God. That's one tumor and rat for each city where the Ark was stored. What do you think the gold tumors looked like? [**Your guess is as good as mine. My son Micah said, "Like a blob with a whole bunch of tubes coming out of it."**]

They secured the five gold rats, the five gold tumors, and the Ark on the new cart. Then they hitched up the two cows, slapped them on the rump, and let the mess go. Had the cows ever pulled a cart before? [**No**] Had the cows ever pulled a cart before? [**No**] Did the cows have calves they wanted to run back to? [**Yes**]

What do you think the cows did? 1 Samuel 6:12 says, *"Sure enough, the cows went straight along the road toward Beth-shemesh."* [**The first town in Israel, NLT**] The cows didn't go back to their calves in the barn. They didn't fight, and they didn't get lost. They went straight to Israel and took the Ark back to God's people.

What present would have been better than gold tumors and rats? If you received a gold tumor for Christmas, what would you do with it?

The Bible says the tumors and rats were given to God as "a guilt offering." They could have saved their money. God just wants what is His. He wants us.

So, What Should I Do?
GO HOME TO GOD

God did what was necessary to encourage the Philistines to give the Ark back. When you and I run away, He's going to do everything He can to bring us back.

Ephesians 2:10 says, "We are God's masterpiece." A masterpiece is something you create that has a bit of you in it. It could be a story, a painting, a Lego castle, or a poem. It's valuable to you, because a part of you is in it.

Maybe you've blown it. You wandered away from God and now realize His plan is best. So go home to God. He isn't mad at you — He misses you. God wants His masterpiece back. His masterpiece is you.

Where else is this taught?

Psalms 51:16-17 (NLT) You do not desire a sacrifice, or I would offer one. You do not want a burnt offering. The sacrifice you desire is a broken spirit. You will not reject a broken and repentant heart, O God.

Ezekiel 18:21-23 (NLT) But if wicked people turn away from all their sins and begin to obey my decrees and do what is just and right, they will surely live and not die. All their past sins will be forgotten, and they will live because of the righteous things they have done. "Do you think that I like to see wicked people die?" says the Sovereign LORD. "Of course not! I want them to turn from their wicked ways and live."

Luke 15:3-7 (NLT) Jesus told them this story: "If a man has a hundred sheep and one of them gets lost, what will he do? Won't he leave the ninety-nine others in the wilderness and go to search for the one that is lost until he finds it? And when he has found it, he will joyfully carry it home on his shoulders. When he arrives, he will call together his friends and neighbors, saying, 'Rejoice with me because I have found my lost sheep.' In the same way, there is more joy in Heaven over one lost sinner who repents and returns to God than over ninety-nine others who are righteous and haven't strayed away!"

Ephesians 2:10 (NLT) We are God's masterpiece. He has created us anew in Christ Jesus, so we can do the good things he planned for us long ago.

When the Earth Ate People

The Question:

Dear God, "Why are my relatives such jerks?"

The Passage:

Numbers 16

Do you know what it means to be incensed?
It has the idea of being super-mad. Have you
ever seen someone who became incensed?

. . . .

Sometimes people are jerks. Often those closest to us
hurt us the most. We want to get even. What would
it be like if God defended us? What would it be like
if God used the earth to eat up angry people?

. . . .

MEET THE EARTH'S MOUTH. . .

EFORE WE DISCOVER HOW THE earth ate people, we have to learn about the angry people in our story. Their names were Korah — he's the leader — and Dathan, Abiram and On. How would you like the name On? At least it's easy to spell! Just when Moses thought he was done with jealous people (see "Don't Mess with Little Brother"), Korah, Dathan, Abiram and On showed up. They hid their jealousy until it grew into anger, then bitterness, and then they became incensed. My definition of incensed is a person so mad he begins to act like a jerk.

Do you know enough about Moses to guess why these guys were first jealous of him? Was Moses super smart? [No.] Did he have lots of money or a nice car? [Nope.] Do you have any other ideas?

These guys were jealous of Moses because Moses was the leader of Israel. He was like a king, but he wasn't rich or called king. He ruled over more than two million Israelites. That's like a LOT of people.

[We live in Albuquerque, New Mexico, and it's like two Albuquerques put together. Do you know how many people live in your city? Is this more or less people than live where you live?]

Moses would talk to God, maybe about where to get food, or where they were going to travel, and God would tell him what to do. Moses would come back from talking to God and say, "Hey everybody, we need to go over here next." And off they would go. Moses was in charge. Korah and his three friends didn't like it. They didn't like it one bit. They wanted to be in charge, they wanted power and fame, and they were incensed with Moses.

Korah and his accomplices also were upset with Aaron. Aaron was Moses' older brother and the high priest. In those days, the high priest was kind of like a pastor in charge of all the other pastors. It was an incredibly important position. Korah and his friends wanted Aaron's rank of high priest, and Moses' status of king. They wanted to be the leaders of both the church and the nation. Of course, Korah would have been the real king. The other three were following him. [This often seems to be the way Satan controls people; he wants both spiritual and physical leadership. From Caesar to Hitler to the Antichrist, Satan desires total control.]

When bullies are afraid of those they want to challenge, what do they often do?

Korah and his jealous friends were afraid of Moses and Aaron, so they worked at getting more people on their side. Thugs work best when they're in a gang. They don't want a fair fight. They searched around the two million people of Israel to find others to harass Moses and Aaron. In time, they found 250 people who had money and power who wanted Moses out of the way. Now Korah had over 250 angry, bitter, jealous, important people who were glad to blame Moses and Aaron for all their problems. This would get them in a lot of trouble — be careful who you follow! [In Numbers 16:2 they are called "250 other leaders of the community, all prominent members of the assembly." [NLT]

All 250 people came together against Moses and against Aaron and said, "You've gone too far!" What they meant was, "You think you're so hot! You have too much power! You shouldn't be in charge! God is with all of us. Why are you ruling us? Who do you think you are anyway? We don't want to follow you anymore!"

Then Moses said to Korah and his friends, "No, you've gone too far."

Do you ever fight like this ..."You think you're so big!"

"No I don't. You think you're so big!"

"Do not!"

"Do so!"

Do you ever fight like that with your relatives?

Have you ever been in an argument when you knew you were right, but you couldn't win? That's where Moses was. He couldn't win because Korah was accusing him — of what Korah was doing!

This is how people — maybe even we do this sometimes — try to cover their sins. If someone lies a lot, he or she may accuse you of lying. If they're cheating by reading off your paper, they accuse you of cheating. If you argue with them, you'll never win. It's your word against theirs. When that happens, you have to give the argument to God, and believe He will make things right in His time. You can't win; God can.

Have you ever had a relative, maybe a cousin or sister, accuse you of doing something wrong (like cheating or lying) when they were the ones doing it? How did you feel? What did you do?

Moses knew this was a dangerous time. Incensed people are dangerous. Rather than trying to defend himself, Moses said, "We'll let God decide who will rule Israel."

In the days when Moses and Aaron lived, those who loved God worshipped Him in a building called the Tabernacle. It was a gigantic tent, and they used it as a portable church.

Moses told Korah, "Show up tomorrow morning at the Tabernacle. God will decide if you and your followers should be leading Israel — or if Aaron and I should continue."

Later Moses tried to talk to Dathan and Abiram to try to persuade them to stop following Korah. He knew they weren't the leaders and hoped they would repent. Unfortunately, they refused to talk to Moses. All they wanted to do was lie about him.

Do you remember On? He also was following Korah, but the Bible doesn't mention him again. We don't know what happened to On — which, if you were On, is a good thing. Maybe he realized he was wrong and quit following Korah. It's never too late to turn back when you're doing something wrong.

The next day, Korah and his persecutors showed up at the Tabernacle. His 250-some followers had been saying bad things about Moses and Aaron to their friends, who in turn talked to their friends. Now many of the two million people were starting to believe them. It looked like it was Moses and Aaron against everyone else: two against two million! The people gathered around the entrance to the Tabernacle, pushing in, straining their necks to see what would happen.

God told Moses to tell the people to get away from Korah, Dathan, and Abiram. He did. Everybody backed away. Now Korah, Dathan, and Abiram were alone.

Then Moses said, "If these guys die a natural death, then God isn't on my side.

But, if God does a miracle and the earth eats them alive along with all their belongings, then you will know who has followed the Lord." Moses had just finished speaking when the earth split apart and opened up like a big mouth, ate the three people, and closed its mouth again! Bizarre!

After that, God sent fire down from Heaven, [**Perhaps something like lightening.**] and the fire killed the other 250 leaders who were persecuting Moses and Aaron. This was the day the earth ate people — complaining, jealous people who followed the wrong leader.

**Do you think God was too hard on Korah and his friends?
What would have happened to Moses, Aaron, and the two
million people if God had let Korah and his friends take over?**

God knew if Korah and his friends ruled Israel, they would ruin Israel. When people are incensed, we have to separate from them and find other friends. Otherwise, they will lead us into destruction with them. Of course, the earth almost certainly won't open up and eat us, but we will feel pressured to follow those friends away from God. On had the right idea and it looks like he turned back before it was too late.

So, What Should I Do?
LET GOD DEFEND YOU

You could pray for the ground to open up and eat your mean brother or sister, but somehow, I don't think that is the lesson God has for us in this story.

People will sometimes be jerks to us, and often it's those closest to us that hurt us the most. All the people in this story were distant relatives — from the original family of Abraham. Some people act like jerks because they have been hurt and they want to pass that hurt on to others. Others may be incensed or jealous like Korah, or just following a messed-up friend like Dathan and Abiram. Why people are jerks doesn't matter — if you knew why, they would still be mean. The real question is, "What should you do when a brother or sister or cousin or parent is mean to you?"

Moses continued to live true to God's word, prayed for God's help, told the truth, and let God defend him. If you follow the example of Moses, God will defend you.

Where else is this taught?

Matthew 5:8 (NLT) God blesses those whose hearts are pure, for they will see God.

3 John 1:11 (NLT) Dear friend, don't let this bad example influence you. Follow only what is good. Remember that those who do good prove that they are God's children, and those who do evil prove that they do not know God.

Job 19:26 (NLT) After my body has decayed, yet in my body I will see God!

Proverbs 28:7 (NLT) Young people who obey the law are wise; those with wild friends bring shame to their parents.

Psalms 7:10 (NLT) God is my shield, saving those whose hearts are true and right.

Psalms 59:9 (NLT) You are my strength; I wait for you to rescue me, for you, O God, are my fortress.

The First Hospital Gowns

The Question:
Dear God, "Will I get married?"

The Passage:
2 Samuel 10

Would you like to be married one day?
If so, what kind of person would you like to marry?

. . . .

God knows if you will get married or not. He lives
in what is called "the eternal present." That means
God is still living in the past, He is here now, and
He is living in the future too. He knows what will
happen in the future because He is already there.

. . . .

OFF TO THE FUTURE...

If GIVEN THE CHANCE, WOULD YOU like to know the future, or do you think it is better living without knowing what is coming?

Would it be good to know the future? If you knew the future, you would never be surprised. You could plan well. You would never lose a card game, you would know who would win every sports event on TV, and you could win the lottery and even "predict" the future.

But, if you knew the future, you would never be surprised — and surprises can be fun. You could never have the fun of wondering if you would win a game, or who would win the sports event you were watching. What if you wanted to make it on a team or go to camp, and then saw the future and realized it wouldn't happen? Then you might not even try to make the team or go to camp. But God may have wanted you to learn something by trying and failing. If you saw something bad about to happen, would you dread it, try to change it?

Sometimes not knowing is better than knowing. That may be why God doesn't often tell us the future. [**God did give us some information about the future. He told us He is coming back again, and about some other future events. But He doesn't often give individuals specific future information about their lives.**]

Who are your best friends?
Are they a good influence on you?

If you do get married in the future, I have a good idea what your future mate is going to be like.

Some Bible stories illustrate to us how our friends determine our future. The disciples had a friend called Jesus. Their lives changed because they hung around Him. Jonathan influenced his armor bearer. Samson hung around Delilah, and she sure changed his future! If you want to know what your future mate is going to be like, look at the friends you have today.

Chances are, in our culture, you won't marry someone you don't date first. And, you rarely date someone you aren't friends with first. Your friends determine your future. Here is a fun, true story to illustrate how that works.

Have you ever done something nice for someone else, but they took it wrong? Maybe you did something kind, but it was misinterpreted? If so, you will understand what it was like to be David in this story.

This story occurred when David was king of Israel, around 1000 B.C. If you read "The Crazy Actor," you will remember David had to hide from King Saul. One place he hid was in Moab, which was close to King Nahash [pronounced Na-hash] of the Ammonites. David and King Nahash became friends. When Nahash died, his son Hanun became king. [Hanun is pronounced Ha-noon, which sounds like an old Western. "I'll meet you in the street at ha-noon."]

David wanted to express sympathy to Hanun about his dad's death. Since there was no postal service or Hallmark card store in 1000 B.C., David had to do this the old-fashioned way. He sent some close friends to tell Hanun how sad he was, kind of like a talking sympathy card.

[We still do the same thing today in political circles. We have fancy memorial services for prime ministers or presidents. When our president or prime minister can't attend, he or she will send an ambassador in his/her place.]

Have you ever received bad advice? Have you ever done what someone else suggested and later regretted it?

Hanun had some evil advisors. Evil people expect everybody else to act like them. These advisors said to King Hanun, *"Do you really think these men are coming here to honor your father? No! David has sent them to spy on the city so they can come in and conquer it!"* **[2 Samuel 10:3 NLT]** That's what these advisors would have done if they had been David. But they weren't David, and they were wrong.

Sometimes, even when you are honorable like David, others will twist your motives. The friends David sent were kind people, relaying a message of sympathy to Hanun because his dad had died. Nevertheless, after Hanun listened to his evil advisors, he became convinced David's friends were spies, so he did something shocking.

Have you ever been to a hospital? Do you know what patients wear in a hospital?

Hospitals force you to wear silly, embarrassing gowns. They don't do it to embarrass you; they do it so that if you have a medical need they can work on you quickly. But that doesn't stop the gowns from being embarrassing.

The gowns are like a thin one-piece dress. You stick your hands through the armholes in the front, and then you have to try to tie the straps in the back. That can be difficult without some help. With no clothes on underneath, you want to make sure you have good friends helping you tie it. From then on, if you have to walk somewhere, the back splits apart and your bottom tends to stick out. That's not a pretty sight for whoever has to walk behind you!

Hanun captured David's friends. They held them down and shaved off half of their beards. Hanun's men must have been laughing, because the Israelites were proud of their beards. Then they *"cut off their robes at the buttocks, and sent them back to David in shame."* **[2 Samuel 10:5 NLT]** It's bad enough to be in a hospital wearing a hospital gown, it's way worse to be walking down the street with half a beard and your bottom hanging out the back of your clothes. How would you feel?

When David heard what happened, he was furious. Hanun realized he had angered David, so he hired 33,000 men from neighboring countries to fight against Israel. He fought. He lost. After losing the first battle, he summoned even more troops, only to lose again. Due to following the wrong advice, Hanun lost over 40,000 soldiers to Israel!

So, What Should I Do?
FIND GODLY FRIENDS

If you have friends who continually assume the worst in others, limit your time with them. If they can't accept someone's apology, or they constantly assign negative motives to others, they aren't people to go to in a crisis. They certainly aren't the type of person you would want to marry later.

Will you get married? I don't know. What kind of person will you marry? In all probability, you will marry someone a lot like the friends you choose. Make sure your best friends are godly friends who will give you God's advice. These friends you can trust to tie your hospital robe — or to say, "I do" to, if/when that day comes.

Where else is this taught?

Psalms 1:1-3 (NLT) Oh, the joys of those who do not follow the advice of the wicked, or stand around with sinners, or join in with mockers. But they delight in the law of the Lord, meditating on it day and night. They are like trees planted along the riverbank, bearing fruit each season. Their leaves never wither, and they prosper in all they do.

Proverbs 27:17 (NLT) As iron sharpens iron, so a friend sharpens a friend.

1 Corinthians 15:33 (NLT) Bad company corrupts good character.

2 Timothy 3:13 (NLT) But evil people and impostors will flourish. They will deceive others and will themselves be deceived.

1 John 2:26 (NLT) I am writing these things to warn you about those who want to lead you astray.

Battle of the Four Kings

The Question:
Dear God, "Why do we have to learn so much in church?"

The Passage:
2 Kings 3

Do you go to church? Do you like going? If no one in your family went to church, would you get up each Sunday and find a way to go without them?

I didn't like church when I was young. It was like school. We had to learn all the books of the Bible, in order, with their weird pronunciations. We memorized verses. We even made a model of the Old Testament Tabernacle. OK, that was fun. Still, why go to church? Can't I be a Christian without it?

SKIPPING CHURCH...

A LOCAL CHURCH IS A GROUP of people who believe in Jesus and meet together in order to help each other follow Him. We make friends, worship God, serve together, and challenge each other to be better than we can be on our own. Sometimes we learn from teaching, sometimes from serving.

[One of my favorite parts about church is going on mission trips. Our church just had a well drilled in Haiti, providing a small village with fresh, clean water when before they had none. This would be an impossible project for any one of us to do alone, but as a church, it was great fun and a terrific learning experience.]

It's important to learn in church because God wants to do wonderful things through you. Church is one way God shows us how to trust, understand, and appreciate Him more. God did great things through people like Jonathan, Ehud and Deborah, and He wants to do great things through you too. These people learned about God, so they knew they could trust Him when the going got tough. If we don't learn about God, we won't be able to trust Him. And if we can't trust God, then He can't do wonderful things through us.

> Do you have friends who don't like it when you go to church? What do you say to them? If they were having a problem, do you think they would let you pray for them?

In order to understand the "Battle of the Four Kings," we have to know a bit about the kings.

Joram was king of Israel. He wasn't as far from God as his mom, Queen Jezebel, and Dad, King Ahab, had been, but he wasn't a close follower of God either. King Joram was like the person who thinks being a Christian is OK for someone else, but not for them. Joram might go to church for something special, but he didn't want to follow God. He wanted to live life his own way.

Jehoshaphat was king of Judah. King Jehoshaphat loved God and wanted to follow Him with all his might.

The third king in the story is nameless. The Bible just calls him "The King of Edom," which I think is rather sad, so I'll call him Ed. King Ed was a friend of King Joram of Israel.

Mesha was king of Moab. He did NOT like King Joram of Israel. Sometimes when people don't like us, they want to fight us. Mesha didn't like Joram so much that he went to war against the entire country of Israel!

King Joram asked King Jehoshaphat of Judah and King Ed of Edom to help him fight King Mesha of Moab. They agreed. Joram decided they should attack by going through the wilderness of Edom.

Have you ever been so thirsty your mouth and lips became dry? What is the longest time you've gone without water?

The three kings [Joram, Jehoshaphat, and Ed, NOT the ones we sing about at Christmastime.] traveled for seven days in the wilderness of Edom. They had drunk all the water they brought with them, and could find no place to get more. Everywhere they went the wells were dry. They had run out of water. Their animals were close to death, and if King Mesha found and attacked them now, they would be too thirsty to fight. [The average person can't go longer than a week without water before dying.]

King Joram panicked. "God brought all three of us here together to die!" he whined.

Jehoshaphat asked, "Isn't there a prophet of God here we can ask to help us? He could talk to God and let us know what we should do."

Someone knew that the prophet Elisha lived close to where they were camped, so the three kings went to see him.

Did the king of Israel think to ask God what to do? [No.] Did the king of Edom think to ask God what to do? [No.] Sometimes we get so worried about what is going on around us we need godly friends to help set us straight. Church is a place full of godly friends.

When the three kings arrived at Elisha's house, he wasn't too happy to see King Joram. Joram was still blaming God for their lack of water. Joram hadn't learned that God doesn't punish His people without a good reason or leave them unprotected. Thankfully, since King Jehoshaphat was with them, Elisha spoke to God on their behalf.

Here is what God told Elisha to tell them.

"Dig ditches all over the valley. Tomorrow the valley will be full of water even though you won't see any rain or feel any wind. Even the animals will have plenty to drink. You will defeat Moab besides. This is nothing for God to do!"

The three kings were thrilled! They went back to the valley, all parched and tired, with their skin sunburned and their lips chapped. The kings quickly ordered the soldiers to find shovels and start digging. This was tough work when they were dying of thirst. But the soldiers dug. They dug trenches all over the place!

The next morning, about the time you go to school or church, the valley was full of water. Maybe God had it rain far away and come down a dry riverbed, maybe it came up from an unknown spring, or maybe God just made water from ... nothing. Somehow, God put water in all the trenches, plenty for everyone and all the animals to drink. But — there was war coming.

King Mesha was ready for a fight. He knew where the three kings were camped. He knew the wells were dry and that they should be dying of thirst by this time. When he got up that morning and looked into the valley, the sun was shining across the water. It never entered Mesha's mind that he could be looking at water. There had been no wind. There had been no rain. And because of the morning sun, all the water in the valley looked red. "It's blood!" the Moabites cried. "The three armies starting fighting each other over what little water they had left and killed each other. Look at all the blood! Let's go down and get the plunder! I'm getting a new chariot!"

They didn't worry about having their weapons at the ready, as each soldier wanted to be first to take what he liked best. Have you ever run downhill so fast you couldn't stop? That's what the soldiers were doing. They were going to take whatever they wanted — free! They were running so fast they didn't notice that the blood seemed less red as they got further down the hill. Then some of them saw movement ahead. "That's odd," they thought, "I thought everyone was dead." As they started to slow down, they realized there was an army running UP the hill toward them! The valley didn't look so red anymore; instead, they saw trenches full of water. Oh no! Now they had to try to stop and get back up the hill and find their weapons.

The three kings and their armies chased the Moabites all the way back to Moab.

What was the one decision that saved their lives? [**Asking God for His help.**] Without consulting God, they would have died of thirst or in war in the valley. With God's help, they won the war. Sometime in the past, Jehoshaphat had learned that God cares for those who follow Him, and He answers our prayers.

So, What Should I Do?

LEARN AT CHURCH

Go to church and learn all you can. Find a group of believers that can help you follow Jesus. Make friends, worship, serve, and challenge each other. Learn from the teaching, and learn from the serving. God wants to do great things through you!

Where else is this taught?

Hebrews 10:24-25 (NLT) Let us think of ways to motivate one another to acts of love and good works. And let us not neglect our meeting together, as some people do, but encourage one another, especially now that the day of his return is drawing near.

Acts 2:42-47 (NLT) All the believers devoted themselves to the apostles' teaching, and to fellowship, and to sharing in meals (including the Lord's Supper), and to prayer. A deep sense of awe came over them all, and the apostles performed many miraculous signs and wonders. And all the believers met together in one place and shared everything they had. They sold their property and possessions and shared the money with those in need. They worshipped together at the Temple each day, met in homes for the Lord's Supper, and shared their meals with great joy and generosity — all the while praising God and enjoying the goodwill of all the people. And each day the Lord added to their fellowship those who were being saved.

Pouring Money Out of the Air

The Question:
Dear God, "Why is my sister so stingy?"

The Passage:
2 Kings 4:1-7

If you have a brother or sister, is either of them stingy?
Are you? Would you like to have more money or stuff?

· ·

Sometimes life seems to be falling apart. You feel like
you have nothing left. Yet God says the only thing
limiting what you accomplish is your obedience
to Him. You plus God can do anything!

· ·

LET'S POUR OUT SOME MONEY...

ONE OF ELISHA'S FRIENDS WHO worked with him had a wife and two young boys. Elisha's friend died, leaving his wife without an income. This would have been an especially challenging time to be a single mom. At that time, most of the jobs were jobs for men. Farming, ranching, well drilling, soldiering and construction were some of the more common trades.

Her boys were too young to help by working, yet they were old enough to help their mom around the house, probably around 4 to 8 years old. Mom was stuck, scared, and grieving for her husband.

[Boys could marry as young as 14, girls could marry at 12. This was the minimum age, with most marrying a few years later. Still, not my daughters — I'd want a decade later! This puts the two boys in this story, who were too young to help earn money, somewhere in their preteens at the oldest.]

Mom went as long as she could on her savings, but in time, she ran out of money. She couldn't pay her rent, and had to borrow money for food. When it didn't seem like it could get any worse, it did.

The people she owed money to came to her house. They demanded payment. She had no money to give.

Then they demanded her sons!

They said, "If you don't pay us what you owe us, you will have to give us your sons. They will grow up and become our slaves, and that way you can pay your debt. When we come back, you must either give us your money or your boys!"

And you thought your sister was stingy! Maybe she is. We are all sinners, and that means we are all selfish, wanting to spend our time, talent and money on ourselves. Your stingy sister is selfish, just like the rest of us. As we follow Jesus and learn to become more like Him, we become more generous. Every good gift we have received comes from God. The more we give, the more like God we become. **[James 1:17]**

Have you ever felt stuck? Maybe you had a problem and
felt as if there was no way out of it? That's called a crisis,
and nothing brings us to God faster than a crisis.

Mom went to Elisha and explained her predicament. She had lost her
husband. She had lost her savings. She was about to lose her boys. Going
to Elisha was her way of going to God. She knew if God were going to help
her, He would do it through Elisha.

Elisha asked her, "What do you have in the house?" It was an easy question to answer, as she had sold almost everything of value to pay her bills.

"All I have left," Mom answered, "is a bottle of olive oil."

"Then here is what you do," said Elisha. "Borrow jars, buckets, containers, anything that will hold oil from anyone who will loan their containers
to you. Take these containers inside your house along with your boys.
Then pour olive oil from your jar into the other jars."

This had to sound weird to Mom. Why would you need a hundred buckets to pour out one little bottle of oil? She did as Elisha said. I wonder what it was like — I wonder if she was excited.

Knock, knock. "Hello, I'm Mrs. Jacobson from down the street. I've a favor to ask. We, my boys and I, need to borrow some jars. Well, buckets really, any pots, jars, or containers you might not be using. What's that? Well, yes, it is rather odd; it's a long story. I'm not quite sure how long I'll need them. I hope that's OK. You have what, an above-ground pool you say? Uh, that's OK, just the jars will do. Thanks."

"Who was that honey? I heard you talking about our old pool out back?"

"That was just Mrs. Jacobson, the crazy pastor's wife. Ever since her husband died, she's been acting a bit weird. Get this — she wanted all our old buckets and jars! I thought she might be nuts enough to relieve us of the old pool, but she wasn't that crazy. I gave her all your old Tupperware."

[Yes, I know they didn't have Tupperware back then. Or pools. Just go with me here.]

After collecting all the jars they could, they locked themselves inside the house. She took a bucket and started pouring her jar into the first bucket. She poured and poured. Her little jar filled the entire bucket!

One of her boys brought her another container. She filled it too. Then she filled another container, and another. Her boys kept bringing jars to her, and she kept pouring. Oil came out of her little olive oil jar until they filled every bucket, jar, and dog dish they'd borrowed. Then the oil stopped flowing.

Mom couldn't believe it! Back then, oil was a staple of the economy. They used it for cosmetics, medicine, food, lamp light, religious rites, even as money. This oil was worth thousands of dollars. Mom went back to Elisha and told him what had happened.

"Elisha, it worked! I have every bucket, jar, dog dish, and Tupperware in the village full of oil in my house!"

"Great!" said Elisha "Go ahead and sell the oil, pay your debt, and you and your boys can live on the money that's left over."

So, What Should I Do?
GIVE TO GOD

The only limiting factor in the miracle was mom's obedience. As long as there were more containers, there was more oil. We don't know that anyone offered her a pool, but if they did, don't you know she wished she had brought it home!

Sometimes life seems to be falling apart. You may feel like you have nothing left. Follow the advice of Elisha, figure out what you do have and give it to God. The only limiting factor in what you can accomplish with God is your obedience to Him. He will supply all you need. You plus God can do anything!

Where else is this taught?

2 Corinthians 9:11 (NLT) Yes, you will be enriched in every way so that you can always be generous. And when we take your gifts to those who need them, they will thank God.

James 1:17 (NLT) Whatever is good and perfect comes down to us from God our Father, who created all the lights in the heavens. He never changes or casts a shifting shadow.

Philippians 4:19 (NLT) And this same God who takes care of me will supply all your needs from his glorious riches, which have been given to us in Christ Jesus.

Ephesians 3:20 (NLT) Now all glory to God, who is able, through his mighty power at work within us, to accomplish infinitely more than we might ask or think.

-

The Madman Chariot Driver

The Question:
Dear God,"Why am I scared of stuff when I believe in You?"

The Passage:
2 Kings 9

Do you remember the story of Elijah and the prophets of Baal? Do you remember that someone was irate at Elijah for what he had done? What was her name? [Queen Jezebel]

· ·

It's possible to trust and obey God when we're frightened. Even Jesus was troubled before going to the cross. Being scared isn't sin. When we conquer our fear and obey God, in spite of our fear, that's obedience. And obedience results in victory!

· ·

LET'S CONQUER OUR FEARS...

ISRAEL WAS GOING THROUGH AN extremely rough time. Queen Jezebel had killed most of the prophets of God, priests and pastors. The people were worshipping a false God called Baal. Elijah, a prophet of God, challenged the 450 prophets of Baal to a showdown. When it was over, Baal hadn't shown up, but God did and the 450 prophets of Baal died that day. That would be the end of the story except for one person — Queen Jezebel.

Ahab was king, but he wasn't as powerful as Queen Jezebel. Jezebel worshipped Baal, she loved the prophets who died, and she hated Elijah. She was so powerful and terrifying, that when Elijah heard that she wanted him dead, he ran! Elijah, who killed 450 prophets of Baal, who believed in God, ran from one woman. [You can read more about that story in "Bizarre Bible Stories 1."]

Have you ever wanted something someone else had? What was it?

Jezebel scared off God's greatest prophet of the time — Elijah. She not only knew how to run off people she didn't like — she also knew how to get what she wanted. One day King Ahab was pouting. When Queen Jezebel asked what was wrong, Ahab said, "I wanted the farm next to our castle. I tried to buy it; the selfish owner won't sell it. He said it had been in his family for years and he wants to keep it in the family. But I want it!"

Queen Jezebel said, "Don't worry about that farm, Ahab. I'll get it for you." Do you know what she did? Jezebel had the owner of the farm and his sons all killed so she could steal the farm for her husband. You wouldn't want her for your neighbor.

Do you have to obey someone you don't like?

One day God sent a prophet to appoint a new king. The reign of Ahab and Jezebel was finally going to end. Where would God find a person strong enough to go up against Queen Jezebel? Even the great prophet Elijah had run from her. She had killed hundreds of people who believed in God.

[1 Kings 18:4] She coveted power and killed all who got in her way. She was a terrifying tyrant. Who would God find to follow Him against her?

God found Jehu. Jehu was a general in the army. God had a prophet pull Jehu aside; pour oil on his head and say, "God wants you to be the next king!" Pouring oil on Jehu's head was God's way of showing Jehu that God's power was going to flow through him. Jehu could now depend on God to protect him from Jezebel — but would he? Would Jehu be brave enough to confront Jezebel?

When the officers in the army heard the prophet had poured oil on his head, they blew their trumpets and yelled, "Jehu is king! Jehu is king!" There would be no backing out for Jehu now.

Do you know anyone who drives too fast? Do you think it would be fun to ride in or drive a police car and go as fast as you wanted? [YES!]

Jehu said, "If the army is with me then don't go to the castle and tell Queen Jezebel what happened. I want to surprise her!" Jehu wasn't going to run away. He was going to run right at Jezebel.

Jehu got into his chariot, strapped on his seat belt, set the radio for the local Christian rock station, and hit the gas. Actually, his chariot would have looked like a large two-wheeled cart pulled by horses — looking a bit like Santa driving his sleigh on land. Only this was no normal sleigh. Most chariots had one to four horses pulling them. Jehu's was probably a rare six-horse chariot pulled with three pairs of horses. This was an extremely fast chariot — almost impossible to control. It was like trying to fly a jet down a crowded neighborhood street. **[Because he was driving very fast, they knew it was Jehu's chariot. If Jehu lived today, he'd have a Ferrari!]**

There was a lookout standing on the castle tower. He yelled down, "Hey, I see troops coming!" A short time later he yelled, "It must be Jehu — the guy in front is driving like a madman!" **[2 Kings 9:20]**

One of Jezebel's wicked sons went out to confront Jehu. Someone shot him with an arrow, and he fell and died at the neighbor's farm. God made certain Jezebel's son died in the very farm she had stolen.

What do you think will happen to Jezebel?

Jehu rushed up to the castle. He could see Jezebel looking out an upstairs window at him. She was shouting at Jehu, calling him a murderer. Evil people often accuse others of what they have been doing. She had killed more innocent people than anyone alive, and she called Jehu a murderer!

Jehu yelled, "Hey, up in the castle, who is on my side?" A couple people looked out and yelled, "We are!"

"Then throw the queen out the window!" Jehu yelled.

They did! They threw the wicked witch queen, Jezebel, out the window. Then it got gross.

Jehu rode his six-horse chariot over Jezebel's dead body. Later, when they went outside to bury her, there was nothing left. Wild dogs had eaten her. Yuck. First the window, then the chariot, then the dogs — why did God make her death so gross?

God had said Jezebel was so wicked she didn't deserve to be buried. **[1 Kings 21:23]** God was right.

So, What Should I Do?
OVERCOME FEAR WITH OBEDIENCE

For some reason, the prophets of Baal didn't scare Elijah, but Jezebel did. For some reason Jezebel didn't frighten Jehu, but other things would. Just because we believe in Jesus, and we know God is all-powerful, doesn't mean we won't get scared. When someone wants what we have and is willing to hurt us to get it — that's scary!

It's possible to trust God, and obey Him, even when we're frightened. Jonah was scared to go to Nineveh, Daniel was scared to go into the lions' den, and even Jesus was troubled before going to the cross. Being scared isn't sin. It's only when we follow our fear and disobey that it's sin. [Like when Jonah ran away and ended up in the fish.] When we conquer our fear and obey God, in spite of our fear, that's obedience. And obedience results in victory!

Where else is this taught?

Deuteronomy 6:2 (NLT) You and your children and grandchildren must fear the Lord your God as long as you live. If you obey all his decrees and commands, you will enjoy a long life.

Deuteronomy 13:4 (NLT) Serve only the Lord your God and fear him alone. Obey his commands, listen to his voice, and cling to him.

Psalms 111:10 (NLT) Fear of the Lord is the foundation of true wisdom. All who obey his commandments will grow in wisdom. Praise him forever!

1 Samuel 12:14 (NLT) "Now if you fear and worship the Lord and listen to his voice, and if you do not rebel against the Lord's commands, then both you and your king will show that you recognize the Lord as your God."

Ecclesiastes 12:13 (NLT) That's the whole story. Here now is my final conclusion: Fear God and obey his commands, for this is everyone's duty.

A Spy and a Traitor

The Question:
Dear God, "Why is it so hard to believe in Jesus?"

The Passage:
2 Samuel 15-18

What should you do when someone picks a fight with you? Is it ever OK to fight? Is it always being chicken to run away?

. . . .

King David was in many battles, but this story is about a time when God told David NOT to fight. Instead, God told David to run away. Sometimes God's advice isn't what we naturally want to do. But if we follow God's advice, we will be rewarded.

. . . .

NOW LET'S GET THAT REWARD...

THIS STORY HAS FOUR KEY players.

• **King David:** He was the second king of Israel, the best known of all Israel's kings. His kingdom was growing, and things were going well for David. But there was one person who did not like King David at all, one person who was out to get him.

• **Absalom:** [pronounced AB'-suh-luhm] Absalom was King David's son. He was an irate young man who hated his father. He refused to forgive his dad David for mistakes David made when Absalom was younger.

• **Ahithophel:** [pronounced uh-HITH-oh-fel] Ahithophel was King David's most trusted advisor and friend.

• **Hushai:** [pronounced HYOO-shigh] Hushai was another of David's advisors, but less known.

Absalom wanted to take the kingdom of Israel away from his father David. He found a sneaky way to persuade the people to support him, instead of his dad, as king.

Absalom would get up early and wait outside the area where they held court. Some cases needed King David in attendance. If David was late, or busy with other matters, or just sleeping in, Absalom was there. He would say, "If I was king, I would help you. I'd give justice. It's too bad this king doesn't care enough to hear your case."

If David did show up, Absalom still had a way to get people to like him instead of his dad. Here is what he would do:

Farmer Fry might argue, "These careless kids were playing on my land last Wednesday. They started a fire and burnt down my entire barley crop. It would have been worth $5,000 at the market. They need to reimburse me what I lost, and more for my trouble."

Then the kids might say, "It wasn't us. We weren't playing with fire; we were playing "capture the flag" in the fields. It must have been a lightning strike. You remember the storms that rolled through on Wednesday, don't you? We didn't do it."

If David ruled, "There is no proof that the children started the fire, the case is dismissed."

Then, after the case, Absalom would talk alone with farmer Fry. "You were so right farmer Fry. If I were king, I'd make those kids pay double for the trouble they caused you. They and their parents should cough up $10,000. They owe it to you. I'm sure sorry that happened. We need more people like you, not like those careless children. Their parents probably slipped David some money to decide for them. I don't know what's going to happen to our country if David remains king much longer. If I become king, I'll make it right!"

But, if David ruled, "The storms came on Tuesday, not Wednesday. I believe the kids did start the fire. The ruling is for farmer Fry for the amount of $5,000!"

Then, after the case, Absalom would talk with the kids and their parents. "I'm so sorry you lost this case. It was obvious the king was on farmer Fry's side from the beginning. It's wrong — no it's unjust that you should have to pay this fine! It's kids like yours and parents like you who we need more of in Israel. Farmer Fry probably slipped David some money to decide for him. I don't know what's going to happen to our country if David remains king much longer. If I become king, I'll make it right!"

For four years, Absalom worked at convincing the people he would be a better king than his dad. He developed an army of followers. Absalom then left for Jerusalem to go to war against his dad and take over the kingdom. What could King David do?

One choice was for King David to get his army together and defend Jerusalem against Absalom. But, there were a few dangers David wanted to avoid. First, David could win — but that would mean David fighting and perhaps having to kill his own son. Second, David could lose and Absalom might kill David! That's no good either. Finally, if David did stay to fight Absalom, they would have to fight in the city, and many innocent people would die.

It's hard to believe in Jesus when nothing seems to be going right. King David lived before Jesus, so he didn't know to trust in Jesus, but he knew to trust in God. It's hard to trust when God tells you to do something you don't want to do. And that's what happened.

David made another choice. David ran away! David the giant-killer warrior got his army together and ran. Because he trusted in God and ran away, there wasn't a war in the city. This protected many innocent people. King David would not have to fight his son — yet.

Who is your best friend? Who would you trust with an important secret?

Absalom marched into town without a fight and took the throne from his father, King David. Now he was King Absalom! He was happy. He was proud. David had left two of his advisors back in the city. Do you remember what their names were? [If you remember those names, you're a genius!]

Ahithophel had been David's most trusted advisor and friend. His advice was the wisest, best advice available. It seemed like he couldn't give bad advice even if he wanted to. Now Ahithophel was David's worst enemy. Ahithophel said to himself, "Self," he said, "I'm going to serve Absalom. I want to be on the winning side. I never liked David anyway, and the fool thought I was his friend!"

What would be fun about being a spy? What would be difficult?

David had another advisor who also stayed back. Hushai was as tough as a jawbreaker and loyal to David too. Hushai stayed back to give Absalom bad advice and to spy for David. He knew if Absalom found out what he was doing, Absalom wouldn't hesitate to kill him. This was his first spy assignment. It was nerve-racking.

Meanwhile David and his army were sad, disorganized, and in great danger.

When you need good advice, whom do you ask?

Absalom brought both Ahithophel and Hushai into his new throne room, and asked each one what he should do. The advice couldn't have been more different.

Ahithophel, the traitor, said, "Oh, Great King Absalom, this is the time to get your army together and attack your dad. Go right now — don't waste a minute! Your father is running down the roads. He's unprotected. He's crying. His army feels defeat in their bones. They're not ready to fight. Let's go! Go! Go! Get 'em and kill 'em before you lose the chance!"

Was this good advice? Yes, for wicked King Absalom it was the right advice. It was the best advice for killing King David.

Then Hushai, the spy, spoke up and said, "Oh King Absalom, that sounds like good advice. Nevertheless, remember your dad is a powerful warrior and he alone was able to kill the great Goliath. He has warriors with him just waiting for a fight. You kicked them out of their homes and palace and now they are furious. You should give them some time before attacking. Then their anger will have died down and their hunger will have grown, and they will be less prepared for a fight."

Was this good advice? No, for wicked King Absalom it was lousy advice. It was the worst advice for catching and killing King David. It would give Hushai time to sneak information to David that could help him. It was lousy advice for Absalom, but if he followed it, David might live.

What do you think Absalom did? Whose advice did he follow? What would you do?

Absalom went with Hushai's advice. By waiting, he gave Hushai time to sneak information to King David. David and his army were able to prepare for Absalom's attack. They hid in the forest, won the war, and David took back the throne. David later rewarded Hushai for doing what was right. When Ahithophel saw that Absalom ignored his advice, he killed himself. He knew Absalom would lose the war.

So, What Should I Do?
GIVE YOUR PROBLEMS TO GOD

It's often hard to trust God and do what is right. When we first believed that Jesus loved us and died on the cross to rescue us from our sins, we started walking in faith. That was the beginning of trusting Jesus. Then we began to trust Him for our day-to-day living. It may be easier to cheat than study, but we must trust it's better to follow Christ and study. It may be easier to forget God, church, the Bible and just live our lives, but it does not take long to realize that following Jesus is the best way to live. Trust Jesus. It's often hard, but always best.

It was hard for Hushai to trust God would help. It was hard for David to leave Jerusalem. But they both believed, followed God, and were rewarded. The most important time to trust God is when it is the most difficult. When you find it hard to trust, follow the advice of David in the verses below.

Where else is this taught?

[David in all probability wrote Psalms 55 about this experience with
Ahithophel. Here are verses 1-2, 12-13, and 20-22 from that chapter.]

Listen to my prayer, O God. Do not ignore my cry for help! Please listen and
answer me, for I am overwhelmed by my troubles… It is not an enemy who
taunts me — I could bear that. It is not my foes who so arrogantly insult me — I
could have hidden from them. Instead, it is you — my equal, my companion
and close friend… As for my companion, he betrayed his friends; he broke his
promises. His words are as smooth as butter, but in his heart is war. His words are
as soothing as lotion, but underneath are daggers! … Give your burdens to the
LORD, and he will take care of you. He will not permit the godly to slip and fall.
(NLT)

Mark 9:23-24 (NLT) "What do you mean, 'If I can'?" Jesus asked. "Anything is
possible if a person believes." The father instantly cried out, "I do believe, but
help me overcome my unbelief!"

The First Public Bathroom?

The Question:
Dear God, "If You love everyone in the world, why will You destroy all the non-Christians soon?"

The Passage:
2 Kings 10:18-27

Have you ever gone camping? Did you like it?

One thing I love about the Bible is that it doesn't try
to make God fit what we think He should be like.
Instead, it tells us what He is like. Sometimes God seems
loving, and other times, judgmental. Nevertheless,
both actions are good. God is good, all the time.

MEET MARVIN...

IMAGINE YOUR NAME IS MARVIN and you are out camping in the woods. You take a hike and start to smell smoke. "I wonder if someone is camping around here," you think to yourself, and you decide to walk toward the smoke smell. Now you hear crackling and the smoke starts to fill the air. "Oh no," you say to yourself, "someone's campfire has started a forest fire!" As you wander a bit closer, you see flames in the tops of the pine trees. Anxious, you turn around only to realize the fire has spread across the tops of the trees past where you have walked. The fire surrounds you!

You try to run back the way you came, but now the fire has worked its way down to the ground. Not able to go any further, you turn around to see the fire creeping closer in every direction. You see a tree untouched by the fire and start to climb. It's scary, scratchy, and difficult, but you make it to the top of the tree. At first, you can see out, so you yell like crazy and wave your arms. After a few minutes the smoke closes in around you, the fire becomes hotter and louder, and you are helpless.

Unknown to you, there is a forest service station on a hilltop close by. Visiting the forest rangers are some men from the military Air Guard. They have with them a large helicopter. A forest ranger was scanning the fire trying to figure out the best way to put it out when he saw you yelling and waving from the top of the tree.

The aviators jump in their helicopter and race toward you. First, you hear the helicopter, and then you feel the wind as its blades blow the smoke away. A man drops down on a rope from the helicopter to rescue you, but the heat and wind from the fire are making the helicopter unstable. As the man is lowered, he hits other trees, scratching his face, arms, and bruising his body. With broken ribs and a bloody face, he finally reaches your tree.

Grabbing a branch, he reaches out to you, "Here, put this on," he yells over the sound of the helicopter. He hands you a harness. "Put this part around your waist, then latch the carabiner. Let's get out of here!"

"No, I'm OK. Thanks anyway."

"What? You're about to burn up. Put on the harness. We can't stay here much longer."

"Hey, I appreciate all you went through, your bloody arms and busted bones and all, but I'll stay here. That harness wouldn't look good with what I'm wearing. Besides, I like the smell of smoke."

"Put the harness on now! This is your last chance!"

"Calm down! The helicopter is fine for you — but I'll take my chances with the fire. Thank you."

An hour later, Marvin's body is reduced to ashes on the forest floor. That night the TV newscaster begins the broadcast by stating, "Today a small forest fire somehow surrounded a camper named Marvin. What we want to know is why our forest service left him there to die. We had a military helicopter and personnel equipped to rescue him just moments away. I guess the military and the forest department didn't care about Marvin. By not rescuing him, they destroyed him."

Of course, the TV newscaster didn't have all the facts. It wasn't the forest department's fault Marvin wasn't rescued. They did all they could. It was Marvin's fault and his fault alone.

We, like Marvin, don't have to perish; we can ask Jesus to save us from our sins and pull us out of death. God provided the way. He did all He could. That is love! It's not enough to appreciate all He went through. We must accept His rescue.

What is the best-known verse in the Bible? Can you quote it?

The best known verse in the Bible, John 3:16 says *"For God loved the world so much that he gave his one and only Son, so that everyone who believes in him will not perish but have eternal life."* **[NLT]**

The first words say that God loves everyone in the world. In fact, He loves each person so much that He gave His Son, Jesus, to rescue us from our sin. If we believe in Him, it's like Marvin accepting the harness — we won't perish. It follows then, that if we reject Jesus, we will perish. That's our choice, not His.

Do some passages in the Bible bother you?
Does God sometimes seem too violent?

There is a similar question that brings us to our "The First Public Bathroom" story. That question is, "Dear God, if You love everyone in the world, why did You destroy innocent people in the Bible?"

When you read 2 Kings 10:18-27, it seems like Jehu, an Israelite king, killed a lot of innocent people. He brought all the Baal worshipers together to their temple, where he knew they would die. How can that be OK? We wouldn't like it if some new politician brought a bunch of worshipers into their church and then killed them all. We'd call that murder!

Baal was an ancient Canaanite religion that had slithered its way into Israel. This religion taught that Baal was in absolute control over nature. The followers believed Baal gave life to people, their animals, and their crops. If Baal wasn't kept happy, then their crops wouldn't grow and their animals wouldn't reproduce. The happier Baal was, the more food and animals they would have. Of course, they wanted to make Baal happy, so they could be rich in food and animals. So, how did one make Baal happy?

The way to make Baal happy was to kill your children! They believed that by giving Baal a baby, he would give them more crops and animals. They sacrificed their children and did other dreadful things during Baal worship. God told Jehu this had to stop.

God led Jehu to carry out a secret plan. Jehu called a meeting and said, "Let's worship Baal! Wait 'till you see how I worship him! Call all the prophets and priests of Baal, bring all his worshipers, and don't leave anyone out. I'll show you how to sacrifice to Baal!"

The people came in droves. No one who loved Baal worship wanted to miss this special date. The king was going to sacrifice! They packed the temple to capacity, waiting to see what child Jehu was going to sacrifice to Baal.

Jehu didn't sacrifice a child.

Jehu sacrificed them.

Everyone in the temple, all those who had been killing their children and teaching others to do the same died that day. Jehu tore down the idols and the things they used to kill children and worship Baal. And Jehu wasn't done.

God thought what they did stunk, so He had King Jehu convert their temple into a public toilet!

So, What Should I Do?
TRUST THAT GOD IS GOOD

Sometimes when we read the Bible, God seems judgmental and mean. At other times, He seems loving and patient. When it's hard to reconcile what God does with who He is, that may mean we don't know the entire story. That's OK. What we need to do is to trust that God is good, even when we don't understand why He did what He did.

What Jehu did seems horrible, until you realize God was saving the lives of children. There are times when God acts out of judgment and times when He acts out of love. Nevertheless, both actions are good. God is good, all the time.

Where else is this taught?

2 Peter 3:9 (NLT) The Lord isn't really being slow about his promise, as some people think. No, he is being patient for your sake. He does not want anyone to be destroyed, but wants everyone to repent.

2 Chronicles 5:13 (NLT) The trumpeters and singers performed in unison to praise and give thanks to the Lord. Accompanied by trumpets, cymbals, and other instruments, they raised their voices and praised the Lord with these words: "He is good! His faithful love endures forever!"

2 Chronicles 7:3 (NLT) When all the people of Israel saw the fire coming down and the glorious presence of the Lord filling the Temple, they fell face down on the ground and worshipped and praised the Lord, saying, "He is good! His faithful love endures forever!"

Psalms 73:1 (NLT) Truly God is good to Israel, to those whose hearts are pure.

Psalms 145:9 (NLT) The Lord is good to everyone. He showers compassion on all his creation.

Nahum 1:7 (NLT) The Lord is good, a strong refuge when trouble comes. He is close to those who trust in him.

Dead Fred

The Question:
Dear God, "Why not go to Heaven now?"

The Passage:
2 Kings 13:20-21

What do you wear when you go swimming? If you were going to a friend's wedding, and could wear any clothes you wanted, what kind of clothes would you choose?

God is preparing Heaven for you. He also is preparing you for Heaven. As you change and become more like Christ, you become more ready for Heaven. It's a bit like changing into fancy clothes for a wedding. It's time for a change!

TURN PAGE TO CHANGE...

Y OU CAN'T GO TO HEAVEN now because you are wearing the wrong clothes. Heaven is as different from earth as swimming is from a wedding. Our bodies are like our clothes. Now we are wearing earthly clothes. When we go to Heaven, we will change into heavenly clothes. Our earthly bodies don't go with us; God will give us heavenly bodies. **[1 Corinthians 15]**

You wouldn't want to wear a swimsuit to a wedding any more than you would want to take your body to Heaven. One reason not to go to Heaven now is we can't go until our bodies change to heavenly bodies. That won't happen until we die or until Jesus comes back for us.

[It looks like God makes some of our clothes right out of our "righteous acts" (Revelation 19:8). This may be a figure of speech, but it's a cool thought that maybe one reason God still has us alive is because our clothes aren't finished. Maybe God still has grandma in the nursing home because He is waiting for the gold buttons — just one final righteous act to complete the perfect gown.]

Do you think you will see Jesus come back? What do you think that day will be like? Why do you think He is waiting so long to return?

Maybe this person meant to ask, "Why hasn't Jesus come back yet?" Peter answers that question. He says the reason Jesus hasn't come back yet is God wants to give more time for people to believe in Him. God doesn't want anyone destroyed! He also reminds us that God is outside of time. A thousand years to us just seems like a day to Him, so it's just been a couple days in God's time since Jesus was here. **[2 Peter 3]**

If you went to Heaven now, what do you think it would be like? After being in Heaven, would you come back down here if God gave you the chance?

Elisha was one of the most dynamic prophets in history. He fixed bad water and bad kids, predicted the weather, brought money out of the air, cured Naaman of leprosy, and even made an ax float. **[2 Kings 2-4]** But even powerful prophets don't live forever. Elisha died and went to Heaven about 832 B.C. God, though, used Elisha one more time, even after he died.

The Israelites didn't use coffins or cremate the bodies of those who died. Instead, when Elisha died, his friends probably had a service, wrapped his body in a bunch of cloths, put the body in a cave, and rolled a large stone over the opening.

In the spring, groups of Moabite invaders used to invade Israel. The Moabite invaders were gangs that would crash in, and murder and plunder when they found Israelites alone or unprotected. The Israelites were safe enough in their cities, but they weren't safe out in the fields or country-side. One spring, a man in Israel died. (We will call him Fred. The Bible doesn't give us his name.) And now dead Fred's friends had a problem.

They couldn't leave dead Fred in his bed all spring. For one thing, they loved him and wanted him buried in a proper cave. For another, Fred was beginning to smell. They could have burned the body or dug a hole in the back yard, but that wasn't considered the honorable thing to do by the Israelites of the day.

They decided to take a chance with the Moabite invaders. They would take dead Fred's body outside of town, to the tombs. You can imagine the plans they might have made. [The tombs were hand-carved caves into the hills where they would put the bodies.]

"Let's wrap up Fred's body tonight, and leave at first light. Maybe the Moabites will sleep in a bit and we can get back home before they see us."

"Sounds good to me — how much do you think he weighs? The four of us carrying him might be quicker than using the wheelbarrow."

"I say we take all four of us and the wheelbarrow. We can ditch the wheelbarrow if it slows us down. The quicker we get him buried, the better. Let's bring in the pastor and have the service now." [They didn't have pastors exactly as we have now. They might have called a family leader, or a son of the prophets, or priest, any of which could function in a pastoral role.]

They called the pastor. They had the service. They had a hard time sleeping knowing the dangerous day that was coming in the morning.

It would have been even harder to sleep had they known of the surprise that was waiting!

The next morning they loaded dead Fred into the wheelbarrow and headed out of town. One of the friends was watching for raiders as the others jogged ahead with the body. They went as fast as possible, and were just entering the area of caves and tombs when the watcher yelled out.

"I see them! There they are! Just over that hill!"

"Where? I don't see anybody. Whoa, wait, there they are. They've seen us! Here they come!"

"What do we do with dead Fred? We can't just dump him here."

"Quick. That cave. I think it's Elisha's tomb. Let's move the stone, throw him in, and run. Elisha won't mind a little company!"

"Great idea. OK, let's all push the stone together. One, two, three, shove! Nice job. You two grab Fred's feet, I've got his head."

"In he goes!"

Out he came!

As soon as Fred's dead body touched Elisha's bones, Fred came back alive! God used Elisha one more time, even after he died!

"He's moving. Fred's alive! Ahhh. ahhh!"

"Hey, where are you going?" Fred must have yelled, "Wait for me!"

Hopefully at least one of the friends was less frightened and able to help Fred. "Dead Fred, uh, sorry, I mean Fred, Run! The Moabites are coming! Oh stink; we wrapped your legs together in the burial cloths! Hang on."

"Be quick about it, I don't want to die just after coming back alive. Unwrap my arms first would you? That way I can help."

Once-dead-now-alive Fred ran back into town with his friends. He probably came back later with them to close Elisha's tomb. What a wild first day back alive that was!

The Bible tells us of a handful of people whom God raised from the dead. It had to be cool to come back from the dead and to tell all your friends what it was like to be in Heaven and have a heavenly body. The bad part is these people had to leave Heaven and leave their heavenly body when they came back to earth. Even worse, they would have to die all over again one day. At least they knew where they were going!

So, What Should I Do?
MAKE GOD SMILE

When God is ready for you to go to Heaven, He will bring you to Heaven. His timing is best. God has a plan for you, and if you are still breathing, He's not finished with you yet. Shoot, God wasn't finished using Elisha even after he died. We don't need to worry about when we go, pleasing God is the main thing, regardless of where we are.

Paul says it best when he says, *"Whether we are here in this body or away from this body, our goal is to please him."* **[1 Corinthians 5:9 NLT]**

Where else is this taught?

2 Corinthians 5:6-9 (NLT) We are always confident, even though we know that as long as we live in these bodies we are not at home with the Lord. For we live by believing and not by seeing. Yes, we are fully confident, and we would rather be away from these earthly bodies, for then we will be at home with the Lord. So whether we are here in this body or away from this body, our goal is to please him.

2 Peter 3:3-4, 8-10 (NLT) Most importantly, I want to remind you that in the last days scoffers will come, mocking the truth and following their own desires. They will say, "What happened to the promise that Jesus is coming again?" … But you must not forget this one thing, dear friends: A day is like a thousand years to the Lord, and a thousand years is like a day. The Lord isn't really being slow about his promise, as some people think. No, he is being patient for your sake. He does not want anyone to be destroyed, but wants everyone to repent. But the day of the Lord will come as unexpectedly as a thief. Then the heavens will pass away with a terrible noise, and the very elements themselves will disappear in fire, and the earth and everything on it will be found to deserve judgment.

1 Corinthians 15:53-54 (NLT) For our dying bodies must be transformed into bodies that will never die; our mortal bodies must be transformed into immortal bodies. Then, when our dying bodies have been transformed into bodies that will never die, this Scripture will be fulfilled: "Death is swallowed up in victory."

The Deadliest Battle Never Fought

The Question:

Dear God, "Why was I put into existence?"

The Passage:

2 Kings 19

One day, if you have kids, what names would you like to name them? Do you know what those names mean?

God loved you even before you were born. Only He knew who you could become, who you will become, and if you will live out the plan He has for your life. Just imagine what God could do through you!

HERE WE GO...

T HIS STORY COMES FROM THE Old Testament when Hezekiah (HEZ-ih-kigh-uh) was king of Judah. His name means "God is my strength." Cool name, eh? Judah was the southern part of what once was Israel. Hezekiah was a good guy — in fact he trusted in the Lord more than all the kings of Judah either before or after his time. **[2 Kings 18:5]** He knew he was "put into existence" to follow God. As a result, he obeyed what God wanted him to do. He must have spent time reading the Bible, in prayer, and bringing justice to Judah. Things were going well, people were able to go to school, work, and live in safety. God helped Hezekiah to be successful in everything he did. Then came Sennacherib (suh-NAK-uh-rib).

The name Sennacherib means "sin has replaced my brother." This name is NOT cool. To make his name easier to remember, we will call him Snack-a-rib.

Snack-a-rib was king of Assyria. This terrible empire was taking over the world. It seemed like everyone Snack-a-rib attacked, he conquered. He was taking over one nation after another, and now he was at the gates of Jerusalem, capital of Judah.

One day Snack-a-rib said, "I'm close to Judah now. We may as well go to war against them. I want all of their stuff. I'm taking over!" Hezekiah, knowing Judah was no match for the army of Assyria, said to himself, "Self," he said, "if we give Snack-a-rib what he wants, maybe then he won't attack us. If he attacks, we will lose. Many innocent people will die, and then he will take what he wants anyway. We may as well give him what he wants now and then maybe we won't have people die in a needless war."

So Hezekiah talked to Snack-a-rib, who demanded 11 tons of silver and one ton of gold. Can you guess how much money that is? That is over $57 million! In order to give all this gold to Snack-a-rib, King Hezekiah had to give away all the precious metal stored in the temple and the palace. [Gold and silver change in price daily. $57 million is the August 2012 value for a metric ton of gold and 11 metric tons of silver, which is about what Snack-a-rib was given.]

Do you know any mean people? Does giving a mean person what they want typically stop them from being mean?

Snack-a-rib took the money, and then brought his army to Judah anyway! He surrounded the city and decided to try to starve the people into surrender. Most of the cities in that time had walls around them for protection, and Jerusalem had walls as well. The advantage to having walls is it made it hard for an army to attack you without them losing many men in the process. The disadvantage to the walls is that all of the farms, most of your food, and much of your water came from outside the walls. If Snack-a-rib kept his army outside the city long enough, and killed anyone who left the city, in time the people would have to surrender or starve. Neither option sounded pleasant to those living in Jerusalem.

Snack-a-rib tried to make the people in the city panic. He yelled to the people, "You'd better give up! You can't fight against me! I have hundreds of thousands of troops. Maybe if I lend you a few thousand horses you could fight against me. Oh, no, my bad. I forgot. You don't even have a few thousand people to ride the horses. I have hundreds of thousands of troops and you couldn't fight me even if I helped you! Don't let King Hezekiah fool you. You can't win against me! I took over all the other cities, I defeated them and the gods they prayed to, and now I am going to take over Jerusalem too!"

How would you feel if you were Hezekiah? How would you feel if you were someone living in Jerusalem listening to what Snack-a-rib was yelling over the walls?

Then Snack-a-rib's commander yelled, "Hezekiah can't save you from us. His God can't save you either. In fact, the Lord told us to destroy your city, so He is on our side! You had better make peace with us and surrender quietly. That way you can have safety and keep peace. You can stay living at home and not starve. God wants us to take over the city anyway. You people need to listen to me because your king won't listen. I'm trying to save you, not hurt you!"

Now what would you do? Could Snack-a-rib be trusted? No, but don't you rather want to trust him? Is it tempting? The northern part of Israel had already fallen to Assyria, maybe Judah would fall too!

But the people who were listening stayed silent. King Hezekiah commanded them to say nothing to Snack-a-rib and his armies, and they obeyed. Then Snack-a-rib's commander gave a description of how bad it would be for them if they didn't surrender. He told them that after a long siege they would get super hungry. Famine would be the result, and they would end up eating their own excrement and drinking their own urine. Yuck! He also told them that if they surrendered they could get to live and go to a place much like Jerusalem. But, if they didn't surrender they would face certain death. The nation was finally following God. There was success and peace, so why was this happening now? Where was God?

Hezekiah prayed. He was terrified. The Bible says he tore his clothes and put on sackcloth and went to the temple of the Lord. Putting on sackcloth was dressing as if you were already dead. Then he went to the temple, which was like going to church to pray. He was saying, "God, without your help, we are already dead. Please help us!"

[His prayer is considered one of the most beautiful in the entire Bible. I've put it in the "Where Else Is This Taught" section at the end of the story.]

What do you think God did?

God let Hezekiah know that Snack-a-rib would not mess with Jerusalem. He wouldn't shoot even one arrow into the city. He would simply leave. It seemed impossible.

But it happened just as God said.

That night, an angel of the Lord went into the Assyrian army camp and killed 185,000 soldiers. 185,000!

Wow! The Michigan football stadium is the largest in the United States, and it only seats 110,000 people. I live in Rio Rancho, New Mexico, with a population of 87,729. More than twice as many people died that night than live in my entire city! How many live in your city? This is somewhat gross, but it gives an idea of what happened. If you lined up all the dead bodies from end to end, starting in the middle of Los Angeles, California, the line of bodies would reach all the way to San Diego. And it doesn't end there. You could keep lining up bodies all the way to Mexico. And it doesn't end there, then you could turn around and line up bodies almost half way back to Los Angeles!

[Figuring the average height of 5 feet 10 inches for the men who died, they would stretch foot to head to foot for 203.46 miles. It is 126 miles from downtown Los Angeles to the San Ysidro, Mexico, border on Interstate 5.]

The 185,000 soldiers that died went to sleep and didn't wake up. It was a painless way to die, but a shock to everyone that lived.

We don't know how many soldiers lived, but it seems safe to assume there were a lot more dead soldiers than living ones the next morning. When the soldiers that didn't die woke up, they found they were sleeping among 185,000 dead bodies.

Imagine Snack-a-rib waking up the next morning and seeing everybody else in his tent still in bed. "Hey, get up you lazybones! It's time to go kill some Israelites. I SAID, WAKE UP!" Then he would have walked over to shake them awake, only to find out they weren't sleeping. They were dead. Then Snack-a-rib would have gone outside to find dead bodies everywhere.

When Snack-a-rib realized what had happened, what do you think he did?

He broke camp, ran back to Assyria, and stayed there. This was the deadliest battle never fought.

What would have happened if Hezekiah hadn't prayed? What would have happened if someone else were king? If Hezekiah hadn't been born?

God planned Hezekiah's life even before he was born. Without Hezekiah, the nation would have been lost.

So, What Should I Do?
LIVE OUT GOD'S PLAN FOR YOUR LIFE

God brought you into existence because He knew who you could become. He loved you even before you were born. He wanted to give you the chance to give Him glory. You give God glory when you live out the plan He has for your life. Hezekiah saved a city and a nation, and brought God glory by trusting in Him. Just think of what God may do through you. God was Hezekiah's strength. He can be your strength too.

Where else is this taught?

2 Kings 19:15-19 (MSG) "And Hezekiah prayed — oh, how he prayed! GOD, God of Israel, seated in majesty on the cherubim-throne. You are the one and only God, sovereign over all kingdoms on earth, Maker of Heaven, maker of earth. Open your ears, GOD, and listen, open your eyes and look. Look at this letter Sennacherib has sent, a brazen insult to the living God! The facts are true, O GOD: The kings of Assyria have laid waste countries and kingdoms. Huge bonfires they made of their gods, their no-gods hand-made from wood and stone. But now O GOD, our God, save us from raw Assyrian power; Make all the kingdoms on earth know that you are GOD, the one and only God."

Jeremiah 29:11 (NLT) "I know the plans I have for you," says the Lord. "They are plans for good and not for disaster, to give you a future and a hope."

The Giant Killers Meet the Six-Toed Man

The Question:
Dear God, "How many people have You helped?"

The Passage:
2 Samuel 21:15-22, 1 Chronicles 20:4-8

Who is your favorite make-believe character from a book or cartoon show? Why do you like your favorites?

When I was little, I had a saying. "Danny do it." I'd be trying to fix something and my dad would offer to help. I didn't want his help." Danny do it," I'd say. Dad would back off, and Danny would usually break it. God wants one thing from us – to accept His help **[1 Corinthians 5:14-15]**.

MEET SOME GIANTS...

MANY STORIES HAVE MAKE-BELIEVE CHARACTERS. Bugs Bunny is the talking rabbit, Veggie Tales has talking celery, the Chronicles of Narnia has one-legged creatures called "monopods" and The Hobbit has giants. All of these creatures are make-believe characters — except one. Do you know which one is real?

Giants are real! At least they were. There are stories of giants from many cultures around the world. We don't have stories of talking celery and monopods from around the world, but we do of giants. We have some extremely tall people today, but none as large as the giants described in Scripture.

A couple of the more famous "giants" today include Leonid and Andre. Leonid Stadnik from the Ukraine is a little over 8 feet 5 inches tall. Most of the ceilings in our homes are only 8 feet tall, so the top of his head would be taller than the ceiling in your room!

My favorite giant will always be "Andre the Giant" who played Fezzik in the movie "The Princess Bride." According to his official website, Andre was 7 feet 4 inches tall and weighed 500pounds. Andre died in 1993.

[There are online reports of giant skeletons around the world, especially in the Americas and Australia. Some of these reports talk about skeletons with six toes and/or fingers and heights tall as 12 feet. Captain Magellan wrote in the ship's logbook about giants living in South America. This is hard to prove, however, and some scientists dispute the claims. Maybe you will be the first archaeologist to prove the existence of giants!]

I believe giants lived because the Bible tells us they lived. God tells us there were giants living before Noah's flood **[Genesis 6]**. There were also giants when Joshua brought the people into the Promised Land **[Numbers 13]**, and when David was king of Israel **[1-2 Samuel]**. These people were HUGE, not just tall. There are only four giants in the history of the world whose names we know. Their stories and the story of the six-toed man are on the next pages.

Giant #1: Goliath

Do you remember the story of David and Goliath? What happened?

[If you don't know the story, you can find it in 1 Samuel 17.]

When David went to face Goliath, how many stones did he pick up? [**Five smooth stones.**] Why did David pick up five stones when there was only one giant?

Have you ever noticed that bullies don't pick on people their own size? Even when they pick on people smaller than they are, they like to have their friends around. Bullies aren't brave.

The giants the Bible talks about were huge compared to us. Goliath was so large that if he stood under a basketball hoop, his head would be inside the net! [**See "The Crazy Actor."**]

Some of the giants in David's time may have been good people, but these five were criminal. When people become more powerful, they often become selfish and mean. That was true of these giants. They worshipped disgusting gods and even killed smaller people for fun. They were thugs.

God helped David kill the giant Goliath when David was a young man. David picked up five stones, ran toward Goliath, used his sling to hit him in the head with a rock, and then cut off Goliath's head with his own sword!

When David was older, he had to fight the Philistines and their giants again. It was hot outside and the battle went on for hours. David was old and tired. His shoulder ached from swinging his sword. The enemy soldiers kept coming and coming and coming. He knew he was in a dangerous place. If he didn't get out of there quickly, he'd be dead. That's when Ishbi-Benob saw him.

Giant #2: Ishbi-Benob

[Pronounced ish bigh-BEE nahb — but pronounce it any way you want. Who's going to know?]

Here is a fun experiment. Find a broom, a bag, and about eight medium-sized books. [About 7½ pounds worth.] Stack the books in the bag, and put the bag on the bristles end of the broom. Now go to the top end of the broom and see if you can pick it up (keeping it level) using just the far end of the broom. How strong would you have to be in order to pick up that broom with one arm and use it as a weapon all day?

A giant named Ishbi-Benob (we will just call him Ishbi) saw old, tired King David struggling to fight. Ishbi had a spear with a wooden shaft and a brass blade at the end that weighed 7½ pounds — about the same weight as the books on your broom. He was big enough to throw his spear with one arm while swinging his huge sword with the other. Ishbi most likely had a smaller armor bearer in front of him holding high a large shield, so Ishbi could hold the sword and the spear. Ishbi saw old, tired, puny David struggling to fight, and moved in for the kill.

David's good friend Abishai was close by and realized what was happening. Without stopping to think, Abishai ran between the giant and David. Wow, was Ishbi big! Abishai was staring at Ishbi's hairy kneecaps under the shield thinking, "What did I get myself into now?" God honored Abishai's love for David by helping him. In a fierce battle, with God helping, Abishai defeated the evil giant Ishbi. This day God helped King David, Abishai, and all the soldiers in Israel's army by defeating Ishbi.

After that, David's friends decided he was too old to go back into battle. They would fight in his place so their king would be safe. David the giant-killer stayed home during the rest of the war. The problem was — there were still three more Philistine giants troubling Israel! Everyone had expected David, the giant-killer, to keep the country safe, but now he was too old. No one, not even the bravest warrior in the country, wanted to fight these giants.

Giant #3: Saph

What's the silliest name of a town you've heard? Some of my favorites are: Skull Valley, Arizona; Picabo (pronounced Peek-a-Boo), Idaho; OK, Oklahoma; Odd, West Virginia; Bath, Getaway, and Wynot, North Carolina.

If you were on a trip and someone asked you, "Where do you live?" Would you like to answer, "I live in the Pit?" The next town the giants attacked was Gob, which, translated into English means "the pit."

The Philistines believed they could now defeat Israel, because King David was too old to fight. Giant Saph and his group of thugs decided this was the perfect time to march into the town of Pit. Unafraid, they expected to take the city easily. Saph marched into the city, with a young man holding his shield out in front to protect his tree-trunk legs. THUMP. THUMP. THUMP. The people hid in their houses as the giant stomped into the city. Shaking, the men with their swords hid inside their homes with their families. Saph's men smashed through the city, breaking into houses and terrorizing the people. Things were the pits in Pit city.

Suddenly, one man ran out into the street — right in front of Saph and his shield holder. His name was Subbecai. Subbecai believed God wanted him to protect the innocent people of Pit, even if Saph could stomp him like a grasshopper **[Numbers 13]**. Subbecai could feel the ground shake with each step the giant took. Saph was grinning, glad for a fight and wanting to kill. Subbecai started to feel sick.

Subbecai had decided to follow wherever God led, even if it meant death. God honored Subbecai's obedience, and helped him defeat Saph. He too became a giant-killer and saved the people of Pit city. But there were still two giants left.

Giant #4: Lahmi

What's the scariest thing you've ever done? Speak in front of class? Horseback riding? Giving a recital?

Lahmi was Goliath's brother [his younger brother, I assume, 1 Chronicles 20:56]. Lahmi never forgave David for killing his brother in battle. He hated David. Lahmi also was fuming about what happened to Saph in Pit city. The Bible tells us Lahmi was HUGE. Just the handle of his spear was as thick as a weaver's beam. A weaver's beam was about 2-feet thick, like one used to hold up the roof of a house. Lahmi decided to go down to Pit city with his house-beam spear and a fresh army. He would teach the Israelites a lesson!

King David and Subbecai were both out of town. Pit city seemed defenseless. Like Saph before him, Lahmi marched into the city, with a shield holder in front of him. Once again, the people in Pit city heard the THUMP. THUMP. THUMP of a giant walking down Main Street. Once again, the families hid inside their homes. One more time, things were the pits in Pit city.

Elhanan, a friend of King David's, was in town visiting friends. [He lived in Bethlehem.] When he heard what was happening, he ran outside and saw the huge beam-spear resting on Lahmi's shoulder. Elhanan knew anything is possible if you're doing what God wants you to do. He attacked the giant!

Somehow, God helped Elhanan, the beam never touched him, and Elhanan saved the city. God honored his obedience. But there was still one giant left.

[I wish the Bible gave us the details of these battles between the men God helped and the giants. Unfortunately for us, it doesn't. Maybe when we get to Heaven we can find these guys and hear their stories first-hand.]

Giant #5: The Six-Toed Man

This guy had six fingers and toes on each hand and foot. How many fingers and toes did he have all together? What do you think he looked like? Where do you think he bought his gloves? Did his feet smell worse with six toes?

It was in Gath, Goliath's hometown, where the last giant went to battle against Israel. The town of Gath had belonged to the Philistines before King David conquered it. The giants wanted Gath back, and the six-toed man was the giant for the job.

We'll call him the six-toed man, because we don't know his name. The Bible tells us he had six fingers and toes so we know he was huge, even for a giant. He may have been the largest, most dangerous giant of all.

God cared for the people of Gath, so He told King David's nephew, [his brother's boy] Jonathan, to fight the giant and protect Gath. Jonathan could feel his heart pounding. He knew God was calling him to fight the giant, and yet he knew, alone, he was no match for the six-toed man.

When the six-toed giant came to town, he met Jonathan, the five-toed nephew of David. Jonathan didn't know how God would help him — he just knew if God could help Uncle David, Abishai, Subbecai and Elhanan, God could help him too. And He did. Jonathan defeated the six-toed giant man in Gath.

So, What Should I Do?
....
ACCEPT GOD'S HELP

When David was young, he picked up five smooth stones when he went to fight Goliath. He may have done that because Goliath had his four friends, Ishbi, Saph, Lahmi, and the Six-Toed Man with him. Maybe David was ready to fight all five at once, and the other four ran away! When David became old, they said to themselves, "Selves," they said, "David can't stop us now, so there is no one who can stop us!" They didn't realize God defeated Goliath — not David. God just helped David, and God wasn't getting any older!

The question, "Dear God, How many people have You helped?" Seems impossible to answer — but it isn't. Let's count. We know God helped David and his four friends — that makes five. If we add you and me to that, we know God has helped at least seven people. Then 2 Corinthians 5:14-15 says, *"Christ died for all ... He died for everyone so that those who receive his new life will no longer live for themselves. Instead, they will live for Christ, who died and was raised for them."* **[NLT]** The answer to the question is that God has offered His help to everyone, even the giants, because Jesus died for the giants too. Whether or not we accept His help is up to us.

God promises to help you live for Christ!

Where else is this taught?

Philippians 4:13 (NLT) For I can do everything through Christ, who gives me strength.

Isaiah 40:29-31 (NLT) He gives power to the weak and strength to the powerless. Even youths will become weak and tired, and young men will fall in exhaustion. But those who trust in the LORD will find new strength. They will soar high on wings like eagles. They will run and not grow weary. They will walk and not faint.

1 Corinthians 1:25 (NLT) This foolish plan of God is wiser than the wisest of human plans, and God's weakness is stronger than the greatest of human strength.

Ephesians 1:19-20 (NLT) I also pray that you will understand the incredible greatness of God's power for us who believe him. This is the same mighty power that raised Christ from the dead and seated him in the place of honor at God's right hand in the heavenly realms.

2 Timothy 1:7 (NLT) God has not given us a spirit of fear and timidity, but of power, love, and self-discipline.

The Worst Birthday Present EVER

The Question:

Dear God, "Why did my grandfather die and not me when he did nothing wrong?"

The Passage:

Matthew 14:1-12

How many things do you think you have done wrong? What is the worst thing you have done? What is the best?

....

It's impossible to know why God lets one person die while others live longer. It definitely doesn't have anything to do with how much good or bad we do in life. Some people who live bad lives, like Hitler, live to middle age. Others who haven't had a chance to do many bad things die when they are young.

....

WHAT GRANDPA WOULD SAY...

If THE PERSON WHO ASKED THIS question were able to go to Heaven and ask her/his grandpa, "Did you ever do anything wrong?" He would laugh. "Of course I did many things wrong! Jesus took all my sins away so I can't remember them all now, but I sinned plenty." Romans 3:23 says, *"Everyone has sinned."* **[NLT]** And Romans 6:23 says that everyone who sins must die. Since you and I, your mom and dad, your grandparents, and everyone else have sinned, we will all die.

There is ONE exception.

Jesus is the only one who "did nothing wrong." Because Jesus never sinned, He is the first human who did not have to die. Instead, He chose to die. Jesus knew that if He, as a good person, died in our place, He could take all our sins away. Jesus gives us his perfect, good life when we trust Him to remove our sins. This makes us right with God. *"God made Christ, who never sinned, to be the offering for our sin, so that we could be made right with God through Christ."* **[2 Corinthians 5:21]**

The result of Jesus choosing to die for us is that we can now have our sins washed away and live forever — even after our bodies die. The full verse of Romans 6:23 reads, *"For the wages of sin is death, but the free gift of God is eternal life through Christ Jesus our Lord."* **[NLT]**

The short answer to the question is that we all must die because none of us is good. The more difficult question is, "Why does it seem that people who do good sometimes die before worse-behaving people?" This story is an example of just that happening.

> ### What is the worst birthday present you can imagine receiving? Do you know who John the Baptist was? What do you know about him?

John the Baptist was a preacher. Baptist wasn't his last name — it was more of a nickname. When people decided to follow his teachings, he would baptize them, so the nickname stuck. He was the cousin of Jesus so they may have grown up as friends.

When John was living, Herod Antipas was the king, and a jerk. Jesus called him a "*fox*," **[Luke 13:31-33]** so we will use that name for him too. The Fox was married. One day he took a trip to Rome to visit his half-brother Philip and his niece, Philip's daughter. Once there, he fell in love with Philip's wife, Herodias! Herodias left her husband Philip, took her daughter, and moved into the palace with The Fox. The Fox then worked on getting a divorce from his wife. This gets complicated, because Herodias also was The Fox's niece.

[Herodias was the granddaughter of Herod the Great; the Fox was the son of Herod the Great. So now The Fox is in love with both his brother's wife and his niece. Yuck.]

The Fox was married, and going through a divorce. The Fox and Philip were half-brothers. Philip was married to Herodias, and they had a daughter. Herodias was the niece of The Fox. Herodias left Philip, moved in with The Fox, and brought her daughter with her. Got it? Good. What a mess.

John the Baptist spoke up and declared that Herodias and The Fox should not be living together. They were married to other people and closely related. John didn't care much about what others thought about him. He said the truth plainly, whether you were the king, or the king's sister-in-law, or the king's niece, or the king's future wife. Herodias was enraged. She had The Fox arrest John.

Herodias wanted The Fox to kill John, but The Fox was more afraid of upsetting the people than he was of upsetting Herodias. Many people liked John, and they would be mad at The Fox if he killed him. It could start a riot where The Fox himself might be in danger. The Fox, who was living a messed-up life, was king. John, who did nothing but tell the truth, was in his prison.

Do you like birthday parties?
What do you like best about them?

On The Fox's next birthday, he had a big, massive, expensive party. When you're king, you can do that. At this party, there was some dancing. His niece, the daughter of Herodias and Philip, was at the party with her mom. She was an amazing dancer. The Fox was impressed. [The Fox may have been drunk and thus speaking foolishly.]

The Fox liked her so much he decided to give her a present on his birthday. He said, "You are such a great dancer; I'll give you whatever you want! You name it, you can have it!" Wouldn't that be terrific? The Fox is a king, with lots of money. Just think of all the things she could ask for! She could ask for a horse or a house or an island or unlimited chocolate forever. Not being quite sure what to ask for, she decided to ask her mother, to get some ideas.

What would you ask for?

Herodias didn't tell her daughter to ask for clothes or chocolate or even for an island. She told her daughter to ask The Fox for — are you ready for this? Are you sure? She told her to ask for the head of John the Baptist on a platter! Yuck! What kind of birthday present is that? Who would want somebody's head for a present? What do you do with a head? What's wrong with her mother?

What was wrong with the daughter? She asked for it! She marched right up to The Fox and said, "I want the head of John the Baptist given to me on a platter." I wouldn't want that girl or her mother mad at me!

Now this worried The Fox. He knew it was wrong. He knew John was simply a preacher telling the truth. He didn't want to kill John, who had done nothing wrong. Nevertheless, he had made a promise. And his party guests had heard the promise he made to the girl.

Because he was afraid of what his niece would say. Because he was afraid of what Herodias, her mother, would say. Because he was afraid of what his party guests would say. He gave her what she asked.

The Fox ordered John, who had done nothing wrong, to be killed in prison. One of his men went to John's prison cell, cut John's head off, and brought it into the birthday party on a platter. He gave it to the girl. The girl gave it as a present to her mother. Yuck.

The Fox did what was wrong. He killed John the Baptist because he was afraid of what others would say if he didn't do it. John, on the other hand, did what was right. He told the truth because he wasn't afraid of what others would say. John honored God. The Fox honored himself. But John is the one who died.

How do you think John's friends felt when they heard he had died? Jesus was his cousin, how do you think He felt? [See Matthew 14:12-13.]

When Jesus received the news that Herod killed His cousin John in prison, He wanted to be alone. It's hard being the one left when someone dies.

We need to remember that sometimes death is a good thing. *"Good people pass away; the godly often die before their time. But no one seems to care or wonder why. No one seems to understand that God is protecting them from the evil to come."* **[Isaiah 57:1 NLT]** Evidently, there are times God takes us to Heaven because He is protecting us from the evil that would have happened to us if we had lived longer.

If we believe in Jesus, we know He is making a new home for us **[John 14:1-3]**. Heaven is a place where there is no more sin, no more tyrants, and we won't carry keys because we won't need to lock our doors. There will be no doctors or hospitals or dentists or needles because there will be no more sickness or crying or death. **[Revelation21:3-4]** When the grandfather in the question at the beginning of this story died, he went to Heaven. Once there, God rewarded him for his service and trust in Jesus. John the Baptist went from prison to Heaven. It's hard on us to see a loved one die, but that doesn't mean it is hard for them.

God decides when and where we are born. We must trust He knows best about when and where we should die.

So, What Should I Do?
LEAVE A LEGACY

Trust that God knows best how long you and your friends and family should live. Follow Jesus, so that, like the grandfather in the question, you will leave a legacy of doing good. Remember you can do what is right — even when the people around you are pressuring you to do wrong. Live like John and honor God without fear of what others might say. Then, when you see Jesus face to face, He will tell you, *"Well done, good and faithful servant!"* **[Matthew 25:21]**

Where else is this taught?

Revelation 21:3-4 (NLT) I heard a loud shout from the throne, saying, "Look, God's home is now among his people! He will live with them, and they will be his people. God himself will be with them. He will wipe every tear from their eyes, and there will be no more death or sorrow or crying or pain. All these things are gone forever."

John 14:1-3 (NLT) "Don't let your hearts be troubled. Trust in God, and trust also in me. There is more than enough room in my Father's home. If this were not so, would I have told you that I am going to prepare a place for you? When everything is ready, I will come and get you, so that you will always be with me where I am."

Hebrews 11:23 (NLT) It was by faith that Moses' parents hid him for three months when he was born. They saw that God had given them an unusual child, and they were not afraid to disobey the king's command.

Acts 5:29 (NLT) Peter and the apostles replied, "We must obey God rather than any human authority."

Romans 5:8 (NLT) But God showed his great love for us by sending Christ to die for us while we were still sinners.

Hebrews 9:28 (NLT) Christ died once for all time as a sacrifice to take away the sins of many people. He will come again, not to deal with our sins, but to bring salvation to all who are eagerly waiting for him.

1 Peter 2:24 (NLT) He personally carried our sins in his body on the cross so that we can be dead to sin and live for what is right. By his wounds you are healed.

Learning Without School

The Question:
Dear God, "Will me not reading the Bible mess me up being a Christian?"

The Passage:
Acts 1-2

If you could know anything, what would you like to know? Why? Wouldn't it be great if you could instantly know stuff without having to study and learn it?

This story is about learning without having to go to school, be home schooled, or even have a teacher! It's about learning without books or having to memorize one thing. It's about learning without studying — awesome!

LET'S SKIP SCHOOL...

AFTER JESUS DIED AND ROSE again, He stayed around Jerusalem for a little while with His disciples and friends. There were about 120 strong followers of Jesus in Jerusalem. They enjoyed spending this extraordinary time with their friend who had come back from the dead. Before Jesus left, He told them that after He was gone, the Holy Spirit would come. This Holy Spirit would help them tell the rest of the world the good news of how Jesus had lived and died and rose again.

[Although 500 people would see Jesus at one time after His resurrection (1 Corinthians 15:6), 120 is the number of followers given in Acts 1:15.]

Do you like saying goodbye?
Why is it hard?

One day Jesus took His followers out for a walk. He reminded them the Holy Spirit would come after He was gone. Then — He left! Jesus raised straight off the ground and went up to Heaven. "Goodbye!" his friends probably yelled. A couple of angels came down from Heaven to talk to them. The angels told Jesus' friends, "One day Jesus will come back just like He left." We are still waiting for that day. Until then, we have the Holy Spirit with us as Jesus promised.

The Holy Spirit is sometimes called "The Advocate." **[John 14:26]** An advocate is someone who helps us. The Holy Spirit is God [that's why He is called "Holy"], unseen [that's why He is called "Spirit"], who comes here to help us. Unseen God, here as our helper — how cool is that?

After Jesus left, the disciples must have felt lonely. It was a pretty small church, with only 120 people. And they were the only church in the world. Jesus had asked them to tell the rest of the world about Him. How could 120 people tell the world about what Jesus had done for them? There were thousands of places to go and languages to learn in order to tell the world about Jesus. There was no Internet, TV, or way to write the Bible in the sky. Worse than that, the Roman government had crucified Jesus, and they were still in power. How could these 120 followers stay safe if they told everyone the Romans had killed an innocent man? How could they travel to the entire world? How could they learn everyone's language? The task Jesus gave them was humanly impossible.

If you were one of the 120 followers of Jesus, what would be your greatest concern?

When is your favorite time to travel? Some people like to see family on holidays like Thanksgiving or Christmas. Others like to take family vacations in the summer. During the time of Christ, Israel had three big travel times each year. One was in the spring [for Passover, around Easter time], another in the summer [for Pentecost, 50 days after Passover weekend], and a final trip in the fall. [Now called "The High Holy Days," around October.] The odd thing about these holidays is that all the Jewish families who took a vacation at one of those times traveled to the same place — Jerusalem!

Jesus rose from the dead on Easter — March/April on our calendars today. He stayed here for 40 days before going back to Heaven just before the Holiday of Pentecost, which comes in early June. People would come to Jerusalem from places as far away as Rome, Egypt, North Africa, and Asia for Pentecost. If you were a super-hero ostrich and could fly from your house in Rome to Jerusalem, you would have to flap your wings for more than 1,400 miles. It was a LONG trip in the days before cars or planes. Still, more people came to Jerusalem than lived there! [The historian Josephus states that as many as 2 million people would come to Jerusalem for the feast days!]

Those who came from different countries spoke different languages and ate different kinds of food. It was entertaining — a little like watching all the different people at the airport. They wore different kinds of clothes and played different kinds of music. You could walk down the street and hear a dozen different languages. It was fun trying to figure out where people were from! Pentecost was a grand time with lots of music at the gigantic temple, new kinds of food, dancing, and fun times with old friends and relatives. The first Pentecost after Jesus left was unique. At this Pentecost, the Holy Spirit showed up!

Jesus' 120 followers were having a prayer meeting. Suddenly, people could see fire coming down around them, but the buildings around them weren't burning. Fire came down on the 120 followers, but they didn't burn either. Instead, the Holy Spirit gave them a special gift. They didn't earn the gift or learn the gift. They didn't have to go to school for it or read books to understand it. The Holy Spirit, in an instant, gave them the ability to speak and understand different languages without ever having to learn them!

The followers of Jesus went to the temple and started talking to people. If the people spoke Egyptian, the believers spoke Egyptian back, even though they had never spoken it before. If the people were from Greece, they spoke Greek. They could speak any language they needed — Latin, Russian, Egyptian, German, Spanish, Aramaic, Hebrew, Greek, Pig Latin — wow, what a gift!

If you could speak another language, what would it be? Why?

That day, because everybody could understand the followers of Jesus speaking in their own language, about 3,000 more people began to follow Christ! Wow! What would it be like if your church grew by 3,000 people in a day? How would that change your church?

Sometime after the feast of Pentecost, people went back to their homes, and they were able to tell their friends and family back home about Jesus. As a result, the followers of Jesus grew from 120 to 3,000 to — well, only God knows how many have believed in Him throughout the years. Today there are over 2 billion Christians. [Current estimate on wikianswers.com]

With the help of the Holy Spirit these early followers wrote the New Testament, traveled, and started churches. When Rome tried to stop them, the Holy Spirit came alongside them and gave them the courage to speak out, love others, and even die for their faith.

Now, 2,000 years later the book they wrote is the best known, most translated, destroyed, quoted, copied, printed, and read book in the world. The entire planet uses the birth of Jesus in order to separate time from BC [Before Christ] to A.D. [Anno Domini ,which in Latin means "The year of our Lord."]. Jesus' followers changed the world by sharing His life through the power of the Holy Spirit. Now, it's your turn. When the Holy Spirit wants to tell the world about Jesus, He tells it. When you need help, He helps!

Will me not reading the Bible mess me up being a Christian?

A Christian is a follower of Christ. The way we know how to follow Jesus is by reading about Him in the Bible. Many of His first followers died to give us this book. Others died in order to get it into our language. God the Holy Spirit thought it was worth their lives to get this information to you. There is no more sure way to follow Jesus than to spend time reading and reflecting on the Bible.

Our sins separated us from God. Since God is perfect, and we are sinful, we can't go to Heaven where He is. If we did, we would bring our sin with us, and then Heaven would be like Earth! Therefore, God put on skin and came down from Heaven for us. He took the punishment for all of our sins when He died on the cross for us.

Now He is making a home in Heaven for us. He will come back to get us when our new home is finished. If you believe this is true, and ask Jesus to rescue you from your sins and become your Lord, then you become a Christian. When Jesus died, He died for you, and He is coming back for you. Do you know how I know this is true?

I know it is true because I read the Bible. The Bible is the primary way the Holy Spirit teaches us what Jesus wants us to do. When I skip reading the Bible, it messes me up as a Christian. It's hard to follow Jesus when I'm not listening to Him.

So, What Should I Do?
· ·
READ THE BIBLE

[One good place to start is the book of John.]

If we skip out on reading the Bible, then the Holy Spirit doesn't have God's word inside of us to work with. You can go to church, pray, and join a youth group, but none of that will impact your spiritual growth like spending time in the Bible.

The difference is a bit like if you had never tasted ice cream. I could try to describe it to you. I could tell you it is cold and smooth and comes in different flavors. But, if I could actually give you a bowl of ice cream for you to eat for yourself — then you would know ice cream. The Bible is the actual word of God, you need to dive in and eat for yourself.

Or think of it another way. You could visit a farm and be shown a beautiful horse. You could brush it, saddle it, and maybe even ride it. Then you would have to go back home. But what if you could actually own the horse and ride it whenever you wanted? Spending time in the Bible is like bringing the horse home, God's Word becomes yours.

The Holy Spirit, who is God Invisible, will help you understand what you read. He can help you tell others about Jesus, too. He may remind you of a verse you had forgotten or give you wisdom you didn't know you had. You will be able to share God's truth, because the Holy Spirit reminded you of it. Maybe, someday, somebody from Armenia will come to your school and try to talk to you. God may just give you the gift of understanding and speaking Armenian in order to share the good news about Jesus with them. Ordinarily we have to learn languages the hard way. We read the Bible and learn slowly. We have the time to do that now. But there are times when God is in a hurry. If you are alive during one of those times, then He can teach you His fast way. When you need help from the Invisible God, He helps!

Where else is this taught?

2 Timothy 1:14 (NLT) Through the power of the Holy Spirit who lives within us, carefully guard the precious truth that has been entrusted to you.

John 14:26 (NLT) But when the Father sends the Advocate as my representative — that is, the Holy Spirit — he will teach you everything and will remind you of everything I have told you.

Acts 1:8 (NLT) "You will receive power when the Holy Spirit comes upon you. And you will be my witnesses, telling people about me everywhere — in Jerusalem, throughout Judea, in Samaria, and to the ends of the earth."

Galatians 3:14 (NLT) Through Christ Jesus, God has blessed the Gentiles with the same blessing he promised to Abraham, so that we who are believers might receive the promised Holy Spirit through faith.

Galatians 6:9 (NLT) Let's not get tired of doing what is good. At just the right time we will reap a harvest of blessing if we don't give up.

Naked Nightmare

The Question:
Dear God, "How are God and Jesus so powerful?"

The Passage:
Acts 19

What do you know about people the Bible says were "demon-possessed?"

The possessed people in the Bible were exceptionally strong. They often hurt both themselves and others. The followers of Jesus didn't run from these people. Instead, they went to the possessed, helping them in the power of Christ. The power of Jesus lives in His followers.

MEET THE DEMON HUNTERS...

Sometimes the Bible talks about demons controlling people. King Saul in the Old Testament had his demons. The chief priest who hired Judas to betray Jesus had his demons — and Judas did too. These people seemed normal, but they did evil things under the control of demons. Some people think evil leaders, like Hitler and Stalin, were demon controlled. The Bible talks about another type of demon-controlled person as well.

There were some people controlled by demons in the Bible who wanted the demons to go away. The Apostle Paul helped these people by making the demons leave. Then the people would be normal again and not hurt others. That's pretty neat, huh?

> **Do you ever play pretend games? Have you ever pretended to be someone else? Who?**
> [Mom. Dad. A superhero. Someone famous.]

As a result of the power God gave Paul to chase demons away, Paul was becoming famous. Some people were jealous of Paul. They wanted to chase demons away too.

Skeva, a leading priest in the town of Ephesus, had a large family with seven boys. These seven brothers wanted to be famous like Paul. They figured, "If Paul can help people by removing their demons, we can too!" The problem was, these seven brothers didn't know Jesus. As a result, God hadn't given them the special power to overcome demons. But that didn't stop them!

They developed a special way to talk to those who were demoniacally controlled. They would say something like, "Through the power of Jesus that Paul talks about, we command the demons to leave." It worked! The demons were leaving, and the brothers were becoming famous. Then a day came that ruined everything for those seven brothers.

> **What was your most embarrassing moment? Have you ever dreamed you went to school and forgot to put on your clothes?**

One day the seven brothers commanded a demon to stop bothering a man. "In the power of Jesus that Paul talks about, go away!" they said. Then the demon answered, "I know about Jesus, and I know about Paul, but who are you?"

Oh no, that wasn't the answer they expected! "Who are we? Uh, we uh, we are, uh, seven brothers." SMASH. TEAR. POW. HIT. RIP.

The possessed man started beating up on all seven brothers at once! He hit them, kicked them, and thrashed them from top to bottom. It was so bad that all seven had to race out of the house to escape the crazy demon. Worse yet they were — are you ready? They were beaten up, bleeding, and — naked! All seven of the preacher's kids ran out of the house without any clothes on! Now they were famous! What an embarrassment! This nightmare about being naked really happened. Had they been real followers of Jesus, this never would have happened.

What made God and Jesus so powerful?

When the townspeople finished laughing, they understood that only God is more powerful than demons. Words don't make you powerful; it's God in you that is powerful.

The Bible begins, *"In the beginning God created the heavens and the earth."* **[Genesis 1:1, NLT]** If someone is powerful enough to make all the stars and galaxies and planets and our earth, that someone is the most powerful being ever. God existed before everything, He never ends, and He is forever young. [Psalms 90:2 says, **"Before the mountains were born, before you gave birth to the earth and the world, from beginning to end, you are God." (NLT)**]

What is true about God also is true about Jesus. The Bible says Jesus didn't become powerful; He always was, is, and will be powerful. Christ is the visible image of the invisible God. He existed before anything was created and is supreme over all creation, for through him God created everything in the heavenly realms and on earth. He made the things we can see and the things we can't see — such as thrones, kingdoms, rulers, and authorities in the unseen world. Everything was created through Him and for Him. He existed before anything else, and He holds all creation together. **[Colossians 1:15-17 NLT]** Jesus is God with skin on.

Nobody made God wise or strong. God is the start, so it is from Him that everything else begins. How is that possible?

Ask your parents; they know everything.

OK, maybe not everything.

But God is as far back as we can go. All the truth of the Bible begins in its first four words, "In the beginning, God."

Have you ever had something valuable you just didn't want anymore? What did you do with it?

When the people in town saw the seven brothers run out of the house bruised, bloody, and naked, they realized God had given Paul a special power. They wanted God to free them from the demons they had been worshipping, so many put their trust in Jesus that same day. They prayed and told Jesus about the evil things they had done and accepted His forgiveness.

The people in this town, who accepted Jesus, still owned a lot of stuff they used while worshipping demons. They knew Jesus wouldn't want them to keep the stuff, but it was worth a lot of money. The Bible says it was worth about "50,000 drachmas." A drachma was worth about a day's wage, or about $212. That works out to about $10.6 million. That's a lot of stuff!

What should they do with all this stuff? They knew they shouldn't give it away or sell it. Then other people would use it to worship demons. So, they burned it — all $10 million worth! They wanted to follow Jesus, and they knew they could not follow Jesus and worship demons.

So, What Should I Do?
FOLLOW JESUS

Genuinely follow Jesus. Let Him live through you. If you only pretend to follow Jesus, don't try to fight demons. You may find yourself running around wondering what happened to your wisdom, your priorities, your life, and your clothes! Follow Jesus. He doesn't make you powerful, He is powerful, and He wants to live through you. Following Him beats any alternative.

Where else is this taught?

Matthew 16:24 (NLT) Then Jesus said to his disciples, "If any of you wants to be my follower, you must turn from your selfish ways, take up your cross, and follow me."

John 8:12 (NLT) Jesus spoke to the people once more and said, "I am the light of the world. If you follow me, you won't have to walk in darkness, because you will have the light that leads to life."

Luke 9:57 (NLT) As they were walking along, someone said to Jesus, "I will follow you wherever you go."

John 10:27 (NLT) My sheep listen to my voice; I know them, and they follow me.

John 12:26 (NLT) Anyone who wants to be my disciple must follow me, because my servants must be where I am. And the Father will honor anyone who serves me.

Colossians 2:6 (NLT) And now, just as you accepted Christ Jesus as your Lord, you must continue to follow him.

The Wedding Story

The Question:

Dear God, "When are You coming back to earth?"

The Passage:

1 Thessalonians 6:13-18, Revelation 19:7-10

If you knew Jesus was coming back one year from today,
what would you do differently in the coming year?
Would you live more Godly or less?

· ·

If I knew Jesus was coming back in a year, I'd be tempted
to go into debt, buy a Ferrari, and leave the earth before
having to pay it back. I wouldn't do it, but I'd be tempted!
Maybe foolish decisions like these are one reason Jesus won't
tell us when He is coming. But be ready – He is coming!

· ·

TIME TO GET MARRIED. . .

J ESUS USED THE JEWISH WEDDING practices of His time to illustrate what His return to earth will be like. If we are going to understand when He might come back, we first need to understand what it was like to be married at the time of Christ. Let's pretend you are a guy living at the time of Jesus, your name is Jethro, **[Exodus 3]** and you want to get married.

How does a guy find a girl to marry in our culture?

"Who should I marry? you might ask yourself. "There's that curly haired girl who talks to me at the synagogue and market. I would LOVE to marry her! She even laughs at my jokes. I need to go through my checklist.

"Is she Cute?" Check. "No, she's beautiful! Is she a Believer? Absolutely, she loves God, that's obvious." Check. "Does she like me? I think so, why else would she laugh at my lame jokes?" Check. "Do I like her name?" Basemath, well, you can't have everything. **[Genesis 26:34]** "Will her parents approve? Will mine?" Ugh, time to go ask. "Hey Mom, Dad, can I ask you a quick question?"

"Sure son, what's up?"

"Well Dad, I was wondering if you were free tonight."

"I am, why?"

"I'd like to ask Basemath to marry me. What do you think?"

"I think your mom and I are going to go talk about it! She's not bad looking, but that name…"

If Mom and Dad approved, you would go to Basemath's house with your dad. Once the family understood why you were there, Basemath and her mom would leave the room. It was time for guy talk. You would have to agree on a few things.

First, Basemath's dad would have to agree for you to marry his daughter.

Second, you would have to pay for Basemath. This was called the "bride price." Her dad would want lots of money, and you and your dad would want to pay less. Once you agreed on the price, you could write a contract and pay for Basemath. Now it's time to get the bride!

[The bride price was not the same as a dowry. A dowry was an ancient custom of a woman bringing money and things into a marriage to help set up the home.]

How does a girl find a guy to marry in our culture?

Enough of the guys. Now let's pretend you are the girl living at the time of Jesus who Jethro wants to marry. You would typically be around 14 to 16

years old. Jethro would come over to your house and introduce himself. Once you knew why he came over to your house, you and your mom would go into a back room while the guys talked.

"I don't know, Mom, what do you think?

"Well, he is a nice boy. He seems to love the Lord. His family is financially well off. You could do worse."

"Yes, but his name, Jethro. He sounds like a hillbilly. And he is the first one to ask. Maybe I should wait for someone better to come along. You know, like that guy with horses and a pool in his parent's back yard."

"You could do that, but once you say 'No,' Jethro will never come back. It's all or nothing."

"How much more time do I have to make up my mind?"

"Let me listen ... it sounds like they've settled on a bride price. You have maybe 10 more minutes! Your dad and I will support you no matter what you decide, but it's your decision now."

If you are a guy, how scary do you think it will be to ask a girl to marry you? If you are a girl, how difficult will it be to answer?

Let's pretend Basemath and her mom come out of the back room. Jethro pours a cup of wine for her. If Basemath drinks it, she is signing the contract by drinking the wine. She and Jethro are husband and wife. If she pushes the wine away, she is saying, "I'll wait for someone better to come along."

For our story, let's assume Basemath drinks the wine. She and Jethro are then legally married, but they aren't living together yet. Before they can live together, a few things have to happen.

[The Bible calls this time betrothal. It's similar to our engagement time, except that the couple is already legally married. It's where Mary and Joseph were in their relationship when she was found to be pregnant by the Holy Spirit. That's why Joseph was thinking of divorcing her. They were married, so he would have to divorce her to end the marriage contract. But, they had not moved in together yet, so he could not have made her pregnant.]

Jethro and his dad will go back home and tell Mom everything that happened. Then Jethro will have to build an addition onto his dad's house. That's where he and Basemath will live during their honeymoon. After the honeymoon, they will move out to a new house somewhere else in town. Just think if you had 10 sons, you would have a gigantic house once they were all married!

While Jethro is building the addition, adding carpet and ceiling fans, Basemath would be busy as well. She has to sleep every night in her wedding clothes and keep a lamp by her bed. She must do this because she has no idea when Jethro and his friends might show up!

Once Jethro's dad tells him the honeymoon addition looks good, then Jethro will ask all his friends for their help. They will pick a night to go "kidnap" Basemath. Like burglars, in the middle of the night, Jethro and his friends sneak up to Basemath's house. Once there, they yell and blow trumpets and beat drums and make a ton of noise, waking up the entire neighborhood. Basemath lights her lamp and comes out. They wake up the entire town in celebration as they continue to make noise on their way to the new addition Jethro built on his dad's house.

They will stay in the honeymoon addition for about a week. After that, they will start the wedding celebration. All their friends will be there; they will sign the wedding album, eat, drink, and have a grand time. After the wedding, they will move into their own house.

OK, I get all that, but what does it have to do with Jesus, and when is He coming back?

The best illustration Jesus could give us about His relationship with us is the Jewish wedding story. In His illustration, He is the groom and we are the bride. That's a bit weird if you are a guy, but it's just an illustration. Get over it!

Like Jethro, the groom in our story, Jesus chose you. He wants to spend eternity with you. Jesus loves you. **[Colossians 3:12, Ephesians 1:4]**

Since we were separated from Jesus due to our sin, Jesus paid the ultimate "bride price," when He died for you. **[Matthew 26, Acts 20:28]**

Jesus is now in Heaven, at His Dad's house. He is adding onto it, making an addition for you. It's going to be a huge house with all those additions! That's why even Jesus didn't know when He was coming back again. He has to wait until God the Father says the room is finished. Then He will come back for us. **[Mark 13:21, John 14:2-3]**

When Jesus comes back for us, He will bring all His friends with Him. He will quietly come down to the earth. Angels and people who have already died and all His friends will be in the air waiting for the signal. When Jesus gives the shout, everyone will make tons of noise, including Michael the archangel and the trumpet call of God! **[1 Thessalonians 4:16-17]**

Then Jesus will bring us to the additions He has been making for us. There will be a wedding reception **[Revelation 19:7-8]**, a wedding album **[Revelation 21:27],** and even a new home to go to when the honeymoon is over. **[Revelation 21:1-5]**

So, What Should I Do?
SAY "YES" TO JESUS

Jesus has done everything the groom could do in order to spend the rest of His life with you, the one He loves. He chose you and paid the "bride price" for you. He wants to make a place for you and come back to get you.

It's up to you whether you want to accept Jesus and live forever with Him, or if you think someone better will come along. We don't drink a literal cup of wine to accept Jesus. Instead, we believe in our hearts Jesus died for our sins and rose from the dead, and we confess aloud that Jesus is our master. **[Romans 10:9-10]** Then, each time they have something called "communion," or "the Lord's Supper," or "The Eucharist" in church, you can remember this story. Drinking the juice is a bit like renewing your vows to Jesus. It's saying, "Yes, Jesus, I believe. I love You and I want to live with You forever." Then stay ready, Jesus could return at any moment! **[Matthew 25:1-5]**

Where else is this taught?

Hosea 2:19 (NLT) I will make you my wife forever, showing you righteousness and justice, unfailing love and compassion. I will be faithful to you and make you mine, and you will finally know me as the Lord.

Romans 10:9-10 (NLT) If you confess with your mouth that Jesus is Lord and believe in your heart that God raised him from the dead, you will be saved. For it is by believing in your heart that you are made right with God, and it is by confessing with your mouth that you are saved.

John 14:2-3 (NLT) There is more than enough room in my Father's home. If this were not so, would I have told you that I am going to prepare a place for you? When everything is ready, I will come and get you, so that you will always be with me where I am.

Mark 13:32 (NLT) "However, no one knows the day or hour when these things will happen, not even the angels in Heaven or the Son himself. Only the Father knows."

1 Thessalonians 4:16-18 (NLT) The Lord himself will come down from Heaven with a commanding shout, with the voice of the archangel, and with the trumpet call of God. First, the Christians who have died will rise from their graves. Then, together with them, we who are still alive and remain on the earth will be caught up in the clouds to meet the Lord in the air. Then we will be with the Lord forever. So encourage each other with these words.

Magic Words

The Question:
Dear God, "Why do You make us wonder?"

The Passage:
Numbers 6:22-27

What do you wonder about? If you could ask
God one question, what would it be?

· ·

God made us creatures that wonder, because He knew
the more we search, dig, and learn the more likely it is
that we will find Him. **[Jeremiah 29:13]** The stars show
His glory **[Psalms 8]**, and even the animals show off
His handiwork. **[Job 40:19]** The more we wonder and
satisfy our questions, the more we learn about God.

· ·

NOW LET'S WONDER...

I WONDER ABOUT SOMETHING NO STUDENT has yet asked me. Maybe I'm weird; you may think this a silly, shallow question, but what I wonder is:

Are there magic words? Do you know any?

I used to love Bugs Bunny cartoons. There is one called "Transylvania" where Bugs is spending the night in a castle with a vampire — only he doesn't know the guy is a vampire. When the vampire sneaks up behind Bugs, Bugs happens to sing "abracadabra" and the vampire turns into a little bat. Bugs sees the bat, thinks it's a large mosquito, and swats him. SPLAT. The bat recovers and flies up, landing upside down on a high ceiling to get away. Just about then, Bugs sings, "hocus pocus" and the bat turns into a vampire again and falls head first to the ground. SPLAT. It's funny [to me anyway] but make-believe. I wonder, are there real magic words?

What makes a word magic? What is magic?

The word "magic" can refer to everything from satanic powers, to illusions a magician uses to entertain an audience. In books like Harry Potter, the characters say magic words, and then their glasses get fixed or a person turns into a rat. Are there really words that can make physical changes?

Yes, words can change things, but I wouldn't call them magic. Magic words are in make-believe stories like Bugs Bunny and Harry Potter. In these stories, the word itself is the magic. Words that are real and can change something physical are what we will call "powerful words." A powerful word isn't powerful because of the word. It's powerful because of what is behind the word.

Creation was like that. God spoke and there was light, water, plants and animals. God didn't build the planet — He spoke it into existence. The words were powerful because God was behind them.

What were the most hurtful words you've heard? What were the most encouraging words you've heard?

Hateful words are powerful. Someone can say hurtful things to you and make your stomach turn. That's making a physical change through words only. You didn't eat something bad, you didn't catch the flu, but you feel sick just the same. The person behind the words made them hurt.

Being told you did something wrong can be a powerful, life-changing experience. When Nathan confronted King David about his sin, David said it felt like his body was wasting away. Nathan never touched David, yet his words physically hurt. **[Psalm 32:3]**

Encouraging words are some of the most powerful of all. They can make us sing inside, they can even help you heal from sickness. **[Proverbs 12:25, 17:22]** The right words can make us work harder, play harder, and live longer. Often the better you know someone the more encouraging you can be. You are the power behind the words of encouragement you speak.

Prayer changes physical things too. When you asked God to take away your sins and become your Lord and Savior, it radically changed things. God removed all your sins. The Holy Spirit came inside you to help you live through your present problems. Jesus began to build a home in Heaven for you. And it doesn't end there.

Every time you pray, something powerful happens. You communicate with the God of the universe, and He chooses to act on your behalf. Every word you give to God is powerful because He loves you and wants to answer your prayers.

There is at least one other kind of powerful word. God calls these words "blessings." The oldest physical copy of part of the Bible we've discovered wasn't written on paper. Inscribed on a roll of silver foil is an ancient blessing from Numbers 6:22-27. It says:

> *Then the Lord said to Moses, "Tell Aaron and his sons to bless the people of Israel with this special blessing: 'May the Lord bless you and protect you. May the Lord smile on you and be gracious to you. May the Lord show you his favor and give you his peace.' Whenever Aaron and his sons bless the people of Israel in my name, I myself will bless them."* **[NLT]**

Did you notice the end? What God promised to Moses seems like powerful "magic." If Aaron and his sons will bless Israel with this special blessing, with these powerful words, then God will bless them. Simply hearing the blessing of God must have changed both how they behaved and how God responded. These words of blessing were a prayer that had the power to change the future.

What does it mean to "be blessed?"

To "be blessed" doesn't mean to be popular, good-looking, or rich. Being blessed means to become all that God designed you to be. We are blessed when we become like Christ. Each one of these Hebrew words of blessing, of helping you become like Christ, is packed with meaning. Here is my paraphrase that I'd like to pray for you.

May the Lord mold you into all that He designed you to be, and may He plant a hedge of protection around you.

May God's face be reflected in yours, and may He bend in compassion to you.

May the Lord look you in the eyes and mend all that is broken in your life.

So, What Should I Do?
BE WONDERFULLY BLESSED

God made us creatures that wonder, because He knew the more we search, dig, and learn, the more likely it is that we will find Him. **[Jeremiah 29:13]** Finding new things about God is a blessing.

This book included 25 stories about wondering. We wondered what made Samson strong, why we get cancer, and if we really need to read our Bible. Wondering is a blessing, because it brings us to God. Here is the favorite lesson I learned while writing this book. It's about a hand, a painting, and a home.

Have you ever wanted to remember something, so you wrote it down on your hand? God uses that illustration to show He won't ever forget you. He says, "I have written your name on the palms of my hands." [Isaiah 49:16, He is writing this about Israel, but it applies to all who are His children.]

Ephesians 3:17 tells us that Christ wants to make His home in your heart.

In the story "God's Masterpiece" we learned that you are like a painting God is creating. **[Ephesians 2:10]**

If we put all these lessons together, we learn that although God could paint a picture of mountains and waterfalls, He chose to paint you. God could live on Mars or Saturn, but He chose to live in you. God could put your name on His calendar and walk away, but God put your name on His hand so He will never forget you. There is no doubt. God loves you.

Be wonderfully blessed. Keep wondering. Let the Lord look you in the eyes and mend all that is broken in your life. Then pray some radical, powerful prayers and watch God work His magic!

Blessings,

Dan

Where else is this taught?

Isaiah 49:16 (NLT) See, I have written your name on the palms of my hands.

Jeremiah 29:13 (NLT) If you look for me wholeheartedly, you will find me.

2 Chronicles 16:9 (NLT) The eyes of the Lord search the whole earth in order to strengthen those whose hearts are fully committed to him.

Matthew 12:37 (NLT) "The words you say will either acquit you or condemn you."

Ephesians 3:17-19 (NLT) Christ will make his home in your hearts as you trust in him. Your roots will grow down into God's love and keep you strong. And may you have the power to understand, as all God's people should, how wide, how long, how high, and how deep his love is. May you experience the love of Christ, though it is too great to understand fully. Then you will be made complete with all the fullness of life and power that comes from God.

Books That Helped

Bible Knowledge Commentary
OT underlying source materials.
Wheaton, Ill.: Victor Books,
Scripture Press Publishers, 1985.
WORDsearch 8 software

Bible Knowledge Commentary
NT underlying source materials.
Wheaton, Ill. Victor Books, Scripture
Press Publishers, 1983.
WORDsearch 8 software

**Egermeier, Elsie E. Egermeier's Bible
Story Book**
Anderson, Ind.
Warner Press, 1955

Enhanced Nave's Topics
NavPress Software, 1994.
WORDsearch 8 software

**International Standard Bible
Encyclopaedia**
WORDsearch 8 software

JFB Commentary
WORDsearch 8 software

**Keener, Craig S. The IVP Bible
Background Commentary**
New Testament. Downers Grove, Ill.
InterVarsity Press, 1993. WORDsearch
8 software

Matthew Henry's Commentary
WORDsearch 8 software

**McDowell, Josh. The New Evidence
That Demands a Verdict**
Nashville, Tenn. Thomas Nelson, 1999

**NAS Hebrew-Aramaic and Greek
Dictionaries**
The Lockman Foundation, 1981, 1998.
WORDsearch 8 software

**Strong's Greek and Hebrew
Dictionary**
WORDsearch 8 software

Teacher's Commentary
Wheaton, Ill.
Victor Books, Scripture Press
Publishers, 1983. WORDsearch 8
software

**The New Greek-English Interlinear
New Testament**
Wheaton, Ill. Tyndale, 1990

The New Unger's Bible Dictionary
Chicago, Ill. Moody Bible Institute,
1988. WORDsearch 8 software

**Theological Workbook of the Old
Testament**
Chicago, Ill. The Moody Bible Institute,
1980. WORDsearch 8 software

**Walton, John H., and Victor
H. Matthews. The IVP Bible
Background Commentary**
Genesis-Deuteronomy. Downers
Grove, Ill. InterVarsity Press, 1998.
WORDsearch 8 software

**W. Murray Severance
That's Easy for You to Say**
Your Quick Guide to Pronouncing Bible
Names. WORDsearch 8 software

Acknowledgments

THIS MAY BE A SMALL book, but it's been a bit of a community project.

Thanks to Camp Pearl Ministries in Reeves, Louisiana, the staff's encouragement and student's energy were the impetus for this book. Don, Angie, the staff, and campers are the best! If you live in Louisiana and haven't gone to Pearl, well that's a bit like living in Louisiana without eating etouffee or buying a 911 Turbo S with automatic shift and cruise control. Why bother?

Thanks to so many at Cottonwood Church — the most real, maybe too relaxed, most wonderful Christian community ever! Thanks especially to Aaron, Debi and the rest of the encouraging editing team. Special mention goes to ultra-editor Geoffrey. I'm still praying you will have a C.S Lewis "most reluctant convert in all NM" experience, so hang on.

Thanks to my sister Janice who tirelessly edits everything I write, while still finding time to publish her own poetry. Check it out at janicecooleyjones.com.

Thanks to my wife JoLynn who puts up with my hiding, writing, bugging her for edits, opinions, and Oreos with Ovaltine. And thanks to our four fun kids Megan, Amanda, Micah and Caleb who are the reason I got interested in kids devotionals in the first place. I can't wait to read them to the grandkids. But don't rush things! First the right person, then marriage, you know…

Thank you Heritage Builders publishing for getting kids into the Bible in creative ways. Thanks for believing in "Bizarre Bible Stories" and taking a chance at re-releasing it in paperback. Thanks for believing in, suggesting, and following through on "Bizarre Bible Stories 2!"

Thanks to God for giving us minds to wonder, stories to ponder, creativity to communicate, and Jesus to follow. Thanks be to God for being good, if not always understandable; for being loving, and correcting us in love; for being just, even when He had to die to pay for our injustice, and for always being gracious even when we are so ungrateful. Thanks be to God.

Author Dan Cooley

I'm senior pastor of Cottonwood Church in Rio Ranch, NM. Cottonwood is a grown up youth group where we study the Bible together, go Jeepin', shooting, rappelling and on missions trips to Haiti. It's great fun and they pay me for it. How great is that?

I started telling little-known Bible stories back when Moses was editing Deuteronomy, at Camp Peniel in Marble Falls, Texas. My four kids grew up listening to these stories, and our desire to pass them on to others brought them into print. The first "Bizarre Bible Stories" has been used for vacation Bible school, mission trips, children's church, camp devotions, and booster seats.

I worked at Camp Peniel for eight years, was a children's and youth pastor for 13 years, and have been playing senior pastor for about 14 years. I have a B.A. in theology from Criswell College and an M.A. in ministry from Moody Seminary. It's amazing who you can bribe these days.

My family and I love Cottonwood Church, Jeepin' and shooting, large dogs, "The Princess Bride," "Napoleon Dynamite," Winnipeg, Manitoba, (where the greatest church in Canada, Elim Chapel, resides and where my kids grew up), green chili, Mexican food and dark chocolate.

I've also written for Leadership Journal and other periodicals, and continue to speak at camps, churches, and youth events. You can contact me through www.danielcooley.com.

And yes, I know Jeepin' isn't a word to the rest of the world. That's why we live in New Mexico.

If You Liked "Bizarre Bible Stories 2," Check Out…

Bizarre Bible Stories
the other kids devotional by Dan Cooley

Get ready for wild, wacky, and weird stories you'd be surprised to find in Scripture… Like flying pigs, walking bones, and 24 other things that really happened!

If you're looking for a predictable children's Bible storybook, don't buy this one. There are no stories about Jonah and the great fish. If you're expecting a story about David and Goliath, you'll be disappointed. A new story beats a rerun every time. You never know what the omniscient God is going to do — unless, of course, you've heard the story before. Find your kids, their pajamas, and a few minutes of time. I promise they (and you) won't be bored.

. . . .

Also published by HeritageBuilders.com,

What Would You Do If…?
101 Five-Minute Devotions for the Family

If you're like many of today's families, you consider "family devotions" a terrific idea. Unfortunately, it's an idea that just doesn't seem to work for you. The kids get bored, your spouse looks at you quizzically, and the whole experiment is quickly forgotten. It doesn't have to be that way!

> "I have one complaint about this book: Greg Johnson didn't write it ten years ago! What Would You Do If…? is a must-read for every parent who is looking for fresh and creative ways to teach values to kids."
> – Kathy Peel
> *Family Circle Contributing Editor*
> *and Author of "Where is Moses When We Need Him?"*